A Guidebook
to the
NEWPORT MANSIONS®

of The Preservation Society of Newport County

Contents

THE
PRESERVATION SOCIETY
OF NEWPORT COUNTY

Welcome

The Preservation Society of Newport County welcomes you to Newport and to the ten historic house museums that it maintains. The Preservation Society was founded in 1945 as a private non-profit educational organization and, through donated funds, gifts, bequests, and loans, is today able to display one of the most extraordinary cross sections of American architecture and interiors in the country. From the Nichols-Wanton-Hunter House, 1748, to the opulent cottages of Newport's "Gilded Age," our houses provide the opportunity to study and appreciate America's rich architectural and artistic heritage of the past 250 years.

Because of its fine climate and island location, Newport grew from an eighteenth-century maritime center into the "Queen of American Resorts." That growth reflects the broad and varied development of America itself, from colonial times through the Industrial Revolution and the exciting era known as the Gilded Age when Newport was the summer home of America's wealthiest and most influential families. Their position and Newport's island charm attracted America's greatest architects and most creative designers, many of whom are represented in the buildings maintained by the Preservation Society.

Our properties provide the opportunity to examine an extraordinary wealth of material, from the fine Newport-crafted eighteenth-century furniture of the Townsend-Goddard cabinetmakers presented at Hunter House, to the early nineteenth-century China Trade objects seen at Kingscote, ancestral collections at Chepstow, and the innovative design of the shingle-style masterpiece

Isaac Bell House. The High Victoriana at Chateau-sur-Mer and the charm of Green Animals, an internationally known topiary garden, are reminders of the creativity of mid-nineteenth-century America. The fine eighteenth- and nine-teenth-century paintings and furnishings of the later revival-style houses such as Marble House, The Breakers, The Elms, and Rosecliff represent museum-quality collections assembled and appreciated by Newport collectors who were committed to improving their young nation's cultural and artistic heritage. Their homes became a reflection of their aspirations and their times, and it was an era when their industrial fortunes built America's greatest museums, universities, churches and public buildings. In the hands of architects like Richard Morris Hunt and patrons such as the Vanderbilts, Newport and America truly entered a "Gilded Age."

The Preservation Society of Newport County is committed to the on-going maintenance and restoration of its properties, seeing them as major links between Newport and America's past.

We hope this booklet will enhance your visit, concisely interpret our properties, and be a pleasant reminder of your visit to Newport.

3

THE BREAKERS

The Breakers is the grandest of Newport's summer "cottages" and a symbol of the Vanderbilt family's social and financial power in nineteenth-century America.

Cornelius Vanderbilt II summered on Ochre Point, a half-mile from Bellevue Avenue, for several years before he commissioned the present building in 1893. Boston architects Robert Swain Peabody (1845–1917) and John Goddard Stearns, Jr. (1843–1917) designed the original house known as The Breakers for Pierre Lorillard. Completed in 1877, the wood and brick house combined a classical symmetrical floor plan with Georgian, Renaissance, and "picturesque" Gothic Revival elements. The small children's cottage on the grounds, designed by the architects of the original house, shows in miniature a few of its characteristics. In October 1885, Cornelius Vanderbilt II bought The Breakers and its site on the Atlantic cliffs of Ochre Point for $450,000. He summered there with his wife Alice Claypoole Gwynne Vanderbilt and their family until 1892, when the house was completely destroyed by fire.

In planning for a new cottage, Mr. Vanderbilt turned to architect Richard Morris Hunt, whose work by this time had contributed to changing the appearance of Newport. Hunt's French Gothic Ochre Court, designed for Ogden Goelet, was Vanderbilt's neighbor to the north on Ochre Point Avenue; his Marble House, designed for Vanderbilt's younger brother William K., was just a short drive to the southwest on Bellevue Avenue. Hunt was little less than official architect to the Vanderbilt family; his houses for them on Fifth Avenue, and elsewhere, had set new precedents in scale and sumptuousness. In spite of his simple tastes and personal modesty, Cornelius Vanderbilt II was patriarch of the country's wealthiest family, a position that made him something of a public figure. If he and his wife were less interested in social competition than the William K. Vanderbilts, the William B. Astors, or others, there was still a position of supremacy to uphold. Richard Morris Hunt welcomed the opportunity to give form to that supremacy in The Breakers.

Cornelius Vanderbilt II was born in 1843, the oldest of nine children of William Henry and Louisa Kissam Vanderbilt. Serious and hardworking, he was a favorite of his grandfather Cornelius, the self-made shipping and railroad magnate whose consolidation of the Harlem, Hudson, and Central New York

The Breakers – Ocean façade

Railway Lines made him America's richest man. The older Cornelius, known as the Commodore, left nearly all of his vast fortune and responsibility for his companies to his son William Henry (one of thirteen children) on his death in 1877. William Henry Vanderbilt had worked his way through the ranks of the New York Central, and his oldest sons, Cornelius and William Kissam, were expected by their grandfather to do the same.

Cornelius II began his working life at sixteen as a messenger for the New York Shoe and Leather Bank; at nineteen he joined the Kissam Brothers banking firm, and at twenty-four he became assistant treasurer of the Vanderbilt-owned New York and Harlem Railroad. Both Cornelius and William were promoted to management positions after the Commodore's death. When their father died in 1885, he left Cornelius and William equal shares of his enormous fortune and the management of the family business. To oldest son Cornelius he also left a gold medal awarded to the Commodore by Congress in recognition of his gift of the

ABOVE, LEFT – *Mrs. Cornelius Vanderbilt II* (Alice Claypoole Gwynne), 1880; portrait by Raimundo de Madrazo y Garreta

ABOVE, RIGHT – *Mr. Cornelius Vanderbilt II*, 1899; portrait by Benjamin Curtis Porter

OPPOSITE – The Great Hall

steamer *S. S. Vanderbilt* to the Union during the Civil War. The medal symbolized Cornelius's new status as head of the family. He became chairman of the New York Central—which held property worth nearly $200,000,000—and a director of forty-nine other railroads. Nine years later, in 1896, when he was 53 years old, a paralytic stroke ended Cornelius's active participation in business. As soon as he could travel, Cornelius was brought from his Fifth Avenue mansion to Newport to recuperate at The Breakers. He died three years later, leaving chairmanship of the New York Central to his brother William.

Unlike his colorful grandfather, Cornelius Vanderbilt II had a reputation for gentleness, fairness, and piety. He met his wife, Alice Claypoole Gwynne, a native of Cincinnati, when they were both teaching Sunday School at St. Bartholomew's Episcopal Church in New York. A vestryman at Trinity Church in Newport and at St. Bartholomew's, Cornelius made deep personal and financial commitments to the church and its mission as well as to several charities, among them the YMCA. Cornelius and Alice Gwynne Vanderbilt had seven children. One, Alice Gwynne, died of scarlet fever at the age of five. Their oldest son, William Henry II, whom Cornelius had hoped would succeed him, died of typhoid fever at twenty-two while a student at Yale; his parents had Vanderbilt Hall built there in his memory. Cornelius Vanderbilt III, Gertrude, Alfred Gwynne, Reginald Claypoole and Gladys Moore Vanderbilt survived their father.

ABOVE – The Breakers – Morning Room

OPPOSITE – The Music Room

When Mrs. Vanderbilt died at eighty-nine in 1934, she left The Breakers to her daughter Gladys, Countess László Széchényi.

In 1948 Countess Széchényi made it possible for The Breakers to be opened to the public as a museum by leasing the house to The Preservation Society of Newport County for a symbolic fee of $1.00 per year. Admission revenues were used in part to finance the restoration of Hunter House. The Countess continued to pay The Breakers' major expenses until her death in 1965. The Preservation Society then leased the house from her heirs, taking on responsibility for its maintenance. In 1973, the Preservation Society purchased The Breakers and its grounds, stable, and greenhouses.

Richard Morris Hunt drew his inspiration for The Breakers from palaces built for the merchant-princes of Genoa and Turin in the sixteenth century. The Italian Renaissance plan was influenced by the work of Andrea Palladio (1508–1580), whose measured drawings of Roman buildings reintroduced the concept of rooms grouped symmetrically around an open courtyard or *cortile*. For The Breakers, Hunt roofed the courtyard, known today as the Great Hall, but maintained the structured symmetry, with rooms of the first and second floors opening onto the forty-five-foot-high central space. Although the Vanderbilts had asked Hunt for a two-story villa, the plan was expanded to four stories, perhaps as much to satisfy Hunt's urge to produce a monumental work as to fulfill the family's requirements. The resulting seventy-room cottage had grand-scale reception rooms on the first floor and bedrooms on the second and third, several of those on the upper story for children. A total of thirty-three rooms were set aside to accommodate resident staff members as well as the maids and valets of guests.

Cornelius Vanderbilt II insisted that the new Breakers be made as fireproof as possible. The steel reinforced masonry structure is sheathed in Indiana limestone. An enormous heating plant beneath the caretaker's cottage was joined to the basement of the house by a wide tunnel. Several hundred tons of coal could be stored at once in the underground boiler room.

The Breakers' main, or west, entrance is approached through wrought iron gateways topped with elaborate scrollwork, including the acorn and oak leaf family symbol, surrounding the initials of Cornelius Vanderbilt II. The thirty-foot-high gateways are part of a limestone and iron fence that borders the property on all but the ocean side. A gravel drive leads to the large carriage porch of the west façade. A rounded bay projects from the south wing, accommodating the huge oval Music Room inside. The most effective elevation is the ocean-facing east façade where the massive north and south wings are joined by a two-story arched loggia in the Palladian manner. Allegorical figures and masks by Austrian-American sculptor Karl Bitter (1867–1915) decorate the arches of the loggias and arcade. Among the smaller cornice decorations are sea motifs and the Vanderbilt monogram. The spacious loggias—the lower one with a vaulted mosaic ceiling and the upper painted to resemble canopies against the sky—were furnished and used as open air extensions of The Breakers' living quarters. The wall between the double loggias and the Great Hall is almost entirely of glass, affording an expansive view of the ocean from inside.

The lofty arches and finely carved classical pilasters of the Great Hall are of French Caen stone. Above the arches are plaques of rare Italian marbles. The oak leaf and acorn motif appears again in the pilasters and their capitals. They support a massive carved and gilt cornice surrounding a ceiling painted to represent the view an open courtyard would have afforded—a blue sky. The freestanding bronze

The Breakers – Library

candelabra are loosely inspired copies of sixteenth-century Italian designs.

The broad grand staircase, with a bronze and wrought iron decorative railing like that encircling the second floor balcony, rises from the hall, breaking into two curving sections at the first landing. The stairwell is dominated by an enormous Flemish tapestry produced from a cartoon by Karl van Mander the younger (1579–1623) in 1619. It is illuminated from above by a multi-colored stained glass skylight thirty-three-feet in length adapted for The Breakers from a skylight created by John La Farge (1835–1910) for the dining room of the Vanderbilts' New York residence and moved to Newport in 1894. On the landing wall is a portrait of Alice Claypoole Gwynne Vanderbilt painted by the Spanish artist Raimundo de Madrazo y Garreta (1841–1920) in the year of her marriage.

Exceptions to the largely Italianate decorations of the Great Hall are two vases of red porphyry set on columns of *griotte brun* marble; they are replicas of a pair in the Salon of Apollo at Versailles.

The Italian Renaissance-style paneling, pilasters, and cornice of the east-facing Morning Room were made in France from designs by Richard Bouwens van der

Boyen (1863–1939). Like the appointments of the Music Room, they were carved, painted, and gilded by Allard and Sons in Paris, then disassembled and shipped to The Breakers for installation. In the corners of the room are eight wall panels depicting the Muses in oil paint on a base of platinum leaf. The mahogany sliding doors are decorated with *grisaille* panels depicting the Four Elements, and the Four Seasons are illustrated in the painted ceiling. The predominant grey and gold of the Morning Room are complemented by its grey Campana marble mantelpiece with ormolu accents and elaborate gilt overmantel. The sixteenth-century-style chairs, settees, and tables are reproductions of pieces in Venice's Palazzo Correr. The suite's gilt and silver leaf surfaces are restored, and the upholstered pieces are covered in rose and cream brocade fabric reproduced exactly from the original silk damask. The same fabric was used for the reproduced draperies.

The adjoining oval Music Room or ballroom is more brilliantly colored and grander in scale but shows the hand of the same designer, van der Boyen. The grey and gold scheme is used again, but here with red Italian cut velvet upholstery and draperies, and more ornately carved and decorated paneling. Massive freestanding columns support the cornice of the curved south wall bay where the grand piano stands. The magnificent bronze and crystal chandeliers, the gilt hardware and the furniture were all designed expressly for the room after

The Breakers – Billiard Room

Italian models. A deeply coffered ceiling, gilt and silver-leafed, surrounds a central allegorical painting depicting Music, Harmony, Song, and Melody.

The library alcove west of the Music Room has dark wainscoting of Circassian walnut decorated with low relief carving and gold leaf; the walls above the wood are covered with panels of gold embossed green Spanish leather. The high Renaissance decorations of the alcove are repeated in the library itself where shelves behind glass doors still hold the books of the Vanderbilt family. The deeply recessed coffers of the walnut ceiling are accented with gold leaf and centered with polychrome insets. The fireplace, unlike others in the house, was not custom-made for it but for France's château d'Arnay-le-Duc three centuries earlier. A bronze bust of William Henry Vanderbilt III, who died while at Yale, is on display in the library, as is a marble bust of his father, Cornelius II. Both are by American sculptor John Q. A. Ward (1830–1910). A bronze allegorical statuette of Labor is one of several pieces in the house executed by daughter Gertrude Vanderbilt Whitney (1875–1942), sculptor and founder of New York's Whitney Museum of American Art.

The billiard room, designed by Richard Morris Hunt, has walls of pale grey-green Swiss Cippolino marble inset with several rare and costly marble varieties. Carved yellow alabaster was used for the arches and mantel decoration. The same material frames the Roman-style ceiling mosaic of a woman and small children in a public bath. A large brass armature supports the room's twin lighting fixtures. The familiar oak leaf and acorn symbol recurs in the room's mosaic floor. Baumgarten of New York was commissioned by Hunt to produce the deep red Santo Domingan mahogany pool table and furniture that contrast dramatically with the cool, subdued marble and mosaic surfaces around it.

The most imposing and richly embellished room in The Breakers is its formal dining room, a two-story space with an area of over 2,400 square feet. Twelve enormous freestanding red and cream rose alabaster columns backed by pilasters of the same material support a massive carved and gilt cornice. Small masks on the ormolu Corinthian capitals echo larger ones on the cornice and the oriels above it where high relief life-size figures, urns, and garlands of fruit are set against murals of classical scenery. The vaulted ceiling rises in carved, painted, and gilt stages to an elaborately framed ceiling oil-on-canvas painting of Aurora, goddess of dawn. Throughout the room a range of gold leaf colors—reds, yellows, and greens—was used. The Renaissance-style fireplace, like the bases of the monumental columns, is of carved and gilt grey marble; its hood of deep grey Cippolino marble is backed by a wall panel of stylized floral designs painted on a ground of silver leaf. On the south wall, a large window faces out to a shell-shaped fountain beneath the grand staircase. The two towering twelve-foot chandeliers were executed by Cristalleries Baccarat, the French glassmakers founded in 1765. Each is composed of thousands

of crystal balls and beads. The twelve matching wall sconces were equipped, like all the fixtures in the house, with gas and electricity in case the newer and less reliable power source should fail. The sixteenth-century-style dining table is of carved oak with lemonwood inlay; it could be extended to seat up to thirty-four. The matching chairs with gilt accents are upholstered in the original red damask, the same fabric as that used for the tasselled draperies.

The paneling of the adjoining breakfast room was made for the Vanderbilts by Allard in the spirit of the Louis XV style. The subdued light green wainscoting with its gilt molding and cornice decoration is an impressive contrast to the prodigious ornamentation of the formal dining room. The delicate mantelpiece is of Italian marble. The mahogany dining suite with carved gilt trim was designed especially for its setting.

Off the dining room is a large butler's pantry with a second-story mezzanine where glass-fronted cupboards hold china and glassware original to the house. The room also contains a warming oven, a safe for silver, and a pair of long scrubbed oak worktables. On the wall over the door is a call-box used by the butler to determine where the attention of the household staff members was required. A narrow room fitted with a large stone sink, originally for arranging flowers, joins the butler's pantry to the huge kitchen.

Bright and spacious, the kitchen with its white tile walls and brown terra-cotta floor was built with no rooms above or around it, to reduce the risk of any kitchen fire spreading to the rest of the house. The original wood and coal-burning stove, more than twenty-feet long, has several ovens and broilers, and an automatic rotisserie. In the center of the two-story space is a long worktable with a zinc-covered top and drawers for utensils along the sides. A huge marble mortar and a chopping block flank the table, and a large collection of polished copper pots and pans hangs over it. The original gaslight fixtures and clock are still in place. Glass-fronted cupboards in the kitchen and flower room hold an unusual collection of iron and copper food molds, many of them made in France. A small, cool, north-facing room off the kitchen was used exclusively for pastry-making; its iceboxes and ten-foot long marble work surface appear just as they did at the turn of the century.

Boston native Ogden Codman (1863–1951), architect and interior decorator, planned the second and third floor rooms at The Breakers in an understated style that makes them dramatically unlike the Italian and French interiors of the first floor. The restrained elegance of these family bedrooms demonstrates the cool neoclassical simplicity Codman would encourage in his book *The Decoration of Houses* (1897), written with novelist Edith Wharton. The thirty-year-old Codman was introduced to Cornelius Vanderbilt II by Wharton at her Newport cottage Land's End, which Codman had remodeled. In his work at Land's End and The

The Breakers – Gertrude Vanderbilt Whitney's bedroom

Breakers, Codman was formalizing ideas that would influence American tastes almost as soon as they appeared in print in 1897.

Alice Gywnne Vanderbilt's bedroom is a streamlined adaptation of Louis XVI models. The moldings and cornice are painted in the original off-white colors and several slightly varying shades of green-tinged cream. The room is one of six Codman interiors restored by the Preservation Society. The reproduced flowered wall fabric preserves the tapestry-like appearance and colors, predominantly coral and beige tones, of the original printed silk and cotton material. The off-white bedroom furnishings in Louis XVI style were made for the house; some of the upholstered pieces are covered in a fabric specially reproduced for them and for the walls of a small adjoining room.

Obviously intended for use as a dressing room for Mrs. Vanderbilt, the neighboring room was used as a bedroom by Gertrude Vanderbilt's husband Harry Payne Whitney while their own Newport house was being redecorated. The room's fabric had deteriorated so that the design had to be pieced together from intact fragments between folds in curtains and near seams in chairs. The pattern of lutes and garlands of flowers was reproduced in the original pinks and greens on a cream ground.

The most vivid of the reproduced fabrics covers the walls of Gertrude Vanderbilt Whitney's bedroom. Because of its eastern exposure, the original wall-covering had faded to a nearly uniform brownish hue, but the cretonne copied from its best-preserved areas has a richly colored pattern of lilacs, tea roses and foliage on a very dark purple ground. Among the room's pictures is a drypoint etching of the young Gertrude Vanderbilt by French artist Paul César Helleu (1859–1927). A bronze figure of an American infantryman borne aloft by an eagle is the work of Gertrude Vanderbilt Whitney. It is a model of her monument to the American Expeditionary Forces who participated in World War I. The sculpture stood atop its seventy-foot pillar at St. Nazaire on the French coast until it was destroyed by Nazi bombing during World War II. Gertrude Vanderbilt Whitney was a prolific sculptor whose frustration at the reluctance of American museums to take seriously the work of contemporary American artists led her to create a series of studios and galleries as showcases of native talent. The Whitney Museum of American Art, which she opened to the public in 1931, grew out of her attempts to gain attention for the work of living American artists.

The bedroom of Cornelius Vanderbilt II is furnished with the carved walnut suite made for him when The Breakers was built. The coral damask bedspread, upholstery, and draperies are of a reproduction fabric nearly identical to the 1895 material. The original gold braid was removed from the old draperies and reap-plied to the new ones. The mantel is of grey and peach Numidian marble.

The bedroom of daughter Gladys, later Countess László Széchényi, has wall panels covered in delicate silk *liséré*. A guest bedroom, the last of the restored Codman interiors, is decorated with the original green canvas panels painted with grey and white neoclassical designs, framed by off-white dado and moldings.

Each of the tiled bathrooms adjoining The Breakers' bedrooms was provided with hot and cold fresh and salt water. Rainwater collected in cisterns and salt water pumped up from the ocean were stored in holding tanks in the attic and fed by gravity to the rooms below. The most magnificent of the bath fixtures is a large white marble tub, carved to resemble a Roman sarcophagus, in Mrs. Vanderbilt's bathroom.

There are two small first-floor rooms flanking The Breakers' entrance hall. One is a modestly appointed gentlemen's reception room with oak paneling. Across the hall is a reception room for ladies. The carved ivory and gilt panel-ing was created for the Mégret de Sérilly townhouse in Paris circa 1776 by the sculptor Gilles-Paul Cauvet (1731–1788). Removed from their original location by Allard, the panels constitute one of the most important Louis XVI interiors in this country. This reception room is thought to be the first French period room installed in an American setting. The nineteenth-century French gilt furniture in

Louis XVI style has upholstery of Beauvais tapestry. The carpet is a subtly shaded nineteenth-century Savonnerie.

The grounds of The Breakers, covering approximately a dozen acres, were originally landscaped by Ernest Bowditch (1850–1918), a student of Central Park designer Frederick Law Olmsted (1822–1903). Pin oaks and red maples line the drive. The formally landscaped terrace is surrounded by Japanese yew, Chinese juniper, and dwarf hemlock. A colorful *parterre* garden on the west terrace was restored more than forty years after the 1938 hurricane destroyed it. Bowditch's original pattern for the garden was determined from old photographs and laid out in pink and white begonia and blue ageratum.

The stable and carriage complex together with greenhouses were built one mile from the villa in 1895. Before a 1970 fire destroyed an upper story, the brick stables had room for twenty-six horses, a variety of carriages, and accommodations for at least a dozen grooms. The Breakers Stable and Carriage House, designed by R. M. Hunt, houses a collection of Vanderbilt carriages, liveries and harnesses. The Carriage Room contains the renowned road coach *The Venture*, driven by Alfred G. Vanderbilt in New York and in England. The greenhouses and their two-acre gardens still provide green and flowering plants and cut flowers for the gardens and interiors of the Preservation Society's houses.

The Breakers is Newport's most frequently visited "cottage." Millions of visitors to the house help make possible valuable preservation and restoration work in buildings owned by the Preservation Society. Its fascination lies partly in its history but mainly in its imposing and magnificent presence.

Gov. William H. Vanderbilt driving road coach *The Venture*, ca. 1930

MARBLE HOUSE

In 1888, William Kissam Vanderbilt asked Richard Morris Hunt to design for him the very best living accommodations that money could buy. Marble House was the result.

Trained at France's École des Beaux Arts, Hunt was committed to classical design principles. His plan for Marble House, derived from that of the Petit Trianon at Versailles, by Jacques-Ange Gabriel (1698–1782), is an academic example of the Beaux Arts classicism that shaped American taste during the 1880s and '90s.

The "cottage" took shape between 1889 and 1892 on a site bordered on the west by Bellevue Avenue and on the east by cliffs overlooking the Atlantic. Marble of several varieties was brought from Europe to a wharf and warehouse on Newport harbor, where Italian stonecutters prepared it for installation. On Bellevue Avenue, wooden fences shielded the construction site from curious onlookers. Newport tradition maintains that men working on different phases of the building were sequestered and forbidden to discuss the project. The William K. Vanderbilts clearly wanted their new summer house to make a dramatic debut and create a powerful impression. It continues to do so today.

The drive to outbuild, outstaff, outdress, and outparty their peers was intense among America's wealthiest families during the 1880s and '90s, and the William K. Vanderbilts were probably the strongest contenders. At 660 Fifth Avenue in New York City they held court in Hunt's version (1880) of the Renaissance château de Blois. Their half-timbered Long Island country house, Idlehour (1878), was an earlier project by Hunt in the "Stick Style." Marble House was another front on which to dazzle the competition. It was Newport's most ornate and expensive summer house, reported to have cost $11 million when it was completed in 1892—a luxurious backdrop for the resort's social dramas. Vanderbilt had already made a present of the cottage to his wife Alva (1853–1933). She was among the first wealthy patrons to demand authentically reproduced period buildings and interiors, especially those inspired by seventeenth and eighteenth-century French models, and she worked closely with Hunt to assure that her marble palace was extraordinary in every detail.

Alva Erskine Smith had begun life in Mobile, Alabama, as an ambitious debutante with more pedigree than money. By 1892 she was one of the foremost hostesses of New York and Newport society, thanks largely to her marriage to William K. Vanderbilt, grandson of the shipping and railroad magnate. Commodore Cornelius Vanderbilt had transformed the ferry business he began

in 1810 with a $100 flat-bottomed boat into a steamship and railroad empire that established his descendants as America's wealthiest family. William K. Vanderbilt, like his older brother Cornelius, for whom Hunt designed The Breakers, and his father William Henry Vanderbilt, served on the board of the family's New York Central and other railroads. An avid yachtsman, William K. co-sponsored a number of America's Cup yachts, including *Defender*, winner of the America's Cup races of 1895. He also sponsored early auto races on Aquidneck Island and Long Island, and he indulged a life-long interest in raising race horses in the United States and France.

Like other summer "cottagers," the Vanderbilts spent a great deal of time traveling at home and abroad, sometimes traversing much of the globe aboard their private yacht. They were usually in New York for most of the winter season, and stayed at Marble House only six or seven weeks of the year. In high season an impressive entourage—a regular staff of thirty-six, including butlers, parlor maids, laundresses, footmen, coachmen, and gardeners—attended the family and their guests. For balls and large dinner parties, extra help was brought in and, like the regular staff, supplied with livery in Vanderbilt maroon.

A family friend described the 1890s as a period of "dazzling wealth, restless endeavor, ambition and rivalry. The 'Gilded Age' had dawned. It merited its name. There was gold everywhere." And Marble House was no exception.

The house's white Tuckahoe marble exterior is a prelude to its richly colored and decorated interiors. Beneath the classical columned portico is a steel entrance grille twenty-feet wide and sixteen-feet high. Between Corinthian pilasters that echo those of the Marble House façade, the grille and its enormous doors have an intricate openwork pattern of gunmetal finish steel over thick glass. Too heavy to be borne on hinges, the one-and-a-half-ton doors turn on pivots set into the frame. The John Williams Bronze Foundry of New York produced the grille from designs by Richard Morris Hunt. In its gilt bronze or ormolu decorations, the architect incorporated Alva Vanderbilt's favorite motif, the sunburst mask of Apollo (symbol of Louis XIV), and plaques monogrammed "W. V."

Just inside the two-story Siena marble entrance hall are two large gilt-framed eighteenth-century tapestries from Gobelins, one of France's renowned tapestry works. Made in 1790 and 1791 respectively, they depict the *Combat of Marcel and Maillard* in 1358 and the *Assassination of the Admiral de Coligny* in 1572. These tapestries, like most of the furnishings on display, are among the original appointments of Marble House. Some European Gothic and Renaissance art pieces were purchased by the Vanderbilts; many more, like the monogrammed bronze lamp standards of the hall, were custom-made for the house. J. Allard and Sons of Paris and New York produced the standards and the bronze fountain with ormolu

Marble House – Dining room

accents that dominates the hall. A monumental Venetian glass mirror hangs over
the bronze fountain.

The grand staircase is of the same yellow Italian marble as the paving and
walls of the hall. Hunt contracted with the New York firm of Batterson & Eisele
for the marble work in the house. The wrought iron and bronze railing of the
stairway and its gilt bronze trophies in the eighteenth century style were made
in Paris by Jules Allard (1831–1907) in 1891 from designs approved by Hunt in
collaboration with Alva Vanderbilt.

The Louis XIV motif is repeated in the ballroom, epitome of what was implied by the term Gilded Age. Its gilt surfaces, green cut velvet hangings, mirrors, and lights prompted a guest in the 1890s to liken it to a jewel box, "far ahead of any palace I have ever seen . . . or dreamed of." The *fleur-de-pêche* marble mantelpiece holds large bronze figures of Old Age and Youth and a mask of Dionysus, all by Allard. Above them, a glass globe of the earth revolves around a smaller celestial globe and tells the month, day, and hour. The mask of the sun god appears again above the mantelpiece mirror. Carved low-relief wood panels by the studio of Jules Allard depicting figures from Greek and Roman mythology surfaced in gold leaf, highlighted by watercolor accents, occupy the walls between the long French windows and glass doors. The twin chandeliers are inspired by fixtures once installed in the château of Maisons Laffitte near Paris. Like all the fixtures in the house, they are fitted for both gas and electricity. In the lavishly decorated ceiling above them, stucco relief panels of classical subjects surround an eighteenth century French painting of Minerva luring a youth away from Idleness.

The dining room is inspired by the Salon of Hercules at Versailles. Its decorative motifs—hunting and fishing—are more subdued, and the room itself, though opulent, is somewhat more restrained than the ballroom. A large oil portrait of Louis XIV attributed to Henri Testelin (1616–1695) over the mantelpiece and a full-length portrait of a young Louis XV by Jean-Baptiste van Loo (1684–1745) on the east wall, boasting its original eighteenth-century presentation frame, dominate the room. In the central ceiling painting, Hermes leads Hebe to Mount Olympus. Two eighteenth-century portraits hang in the room: one depicts Charles III Ferdinand, Duke of Mantua by Hyacinthe Riguad (1659–1743); the other, also by Rigaud, his wife, Suzanne-Henriette de Lorraine, Duchess of Mantua. The walls and classical pilasters are of deep pink Numidian marble from Western Algeria; the capitals, wall sconces, decorative appliques, and lamp standards are of heavy ormolu. The mahogany dining table has elaborate gilt pedestals. The gilded bronze chairs were made for the house in Paris by Allard and are covered in metallic-threaded cut velvet. Footmen were called upon to assist guests with their heavy chairs. Food prepared in the kitchen below was brought by dumbwaiter to a pantry adjoining the dining room.

The large basement kitchen was the province of a French *chef-de-cuisine*, his *sous-chef*, two kitchen maids, and a kitchen boy. The room is fitted out with a massive twenty-five-foot-long, six-oven cast iron coal-burning stove made by Duparquet, Huot & Moneuse of New York, soapstone sinks, built-in iceboxes, and glass-fronted oak cupboards. Menus for many of Newport's most lavish summer parties and dinners—from the August 1892 opening reception to the opening of the Chinese Teahouse in 1914—took shape there. The kitchen was closed after Alva stopped summering at Marble House, but the original equipment, packed away in bins, was well preserved. A full-scale restoration of all the room's elements—from oak woodwork to gaslight fixtures—was completed by the Preservation Society in 1983.

Today the kitchen looks almost exactly as it did at the turn of the century, with polished copper pans hanging from a huge oval rack over a long scrubbed oak work table. The cutting boards, trays, mortar and pestle, ice molds, toasting racks, rolling pins, scales, cutlery, and serving platters used at that time are on display.

The first-floor Gothic Room, entirely different in character from the ballroom and dining room, demonstrates Alva Vanderbilt's studied eclecticism. It is one of several rooms illustrating her favorite French periods from Charles VII to Louis XV—a textbook example of French Gothic decoration complete with characteristic arches, chimneypiece, ribbing, and figurative carving. It was designed to hold a collection of medieval art objects later sold by the family. This room has been restored to its original appearance and features four stained glass windows whose designs incorporate both thirteenth- and nineteenth-century elements. They closely duplicate the dispersed originals.

The paneling, bookshelves and portable stair of the rococo library are elaborately carved of walnut in Louis XV style. Decorations include *grisaille* panels depicting four of the Sciences, and frescoes of Time and History. The oil portrait of the youngest of Alva and William K. Vanderbilt's three children, Harold Stirling Vanderbilt, was painted by French artist Charles Chaplin (1825–1891) when Harold was two years old; it was shown at the Paris Exhibition in 1889.

Among the most notable pieces of commissioned furniture in the collections of the Preservation Society are two black and gold cabinets in the main hall. They are in the style of seventeenth-century French designer André-Charles Boulle (1642–1732), the most celebrated furniture maker of the Louis XIV era. The two cabinet pieces have ebony frames inlaid with tortoiseshell and etched brass and are mounted in ormolu. They are attributed to Beurdeley of Paris, a firm which specialized in high quality interpretations of seventeenth- and eighteenth-century furniture.

Marble House – Library

The two small rooms off the mezzanine reflect the respective interests of William and Alva Vanderbilt. On the walls of Mr. Vanderbilt's office are paintings of his champion racehorses. The kingwood desk and other pieces were made by Henry Dasson (1825–1896) of Paris in Louis XV style, as were the marquetry pieces in Mrs. Vanderbilt's little sitting room opposite. There the white Louis XV Revival woodwork provides an appropriate setting for the eighteenth-century court portrait by J. B. Siméon Chardin (1699–1779).

A copy of seventeenth-century Italian sculptor Giovanni-Lorenzo Bernini's famous bust of Louis XIV by Auguste Edme Suchetet (1854–1932) is opposite the second floor landing. The bust is flanked by medallion relief portraits of Jules Hardouin-Mansart (1646–1708), architect of Versailles, and of Richard Morris Hunt by the sculptor Karl Bitter (1867–1915). The hall ceiling has the mythological themes of the principal first floor rooms. Groups of red and green gilt figures represent the arts, military pursuits, the earth, and the sea.

In Alva Vanderbilt's bedroom, rococo woodwork and furnishings compete for attention. The wood and stucco arabesques and figures of the ceiling and overdoors are repeated in the elaborate custom-made bed inspired by a Daniel Marot (c. 1663–1752) drawing. The lilac damask drapery and wall fabric by the designer Roux has been rewoven for this room by its original maker, the French firm of Prelle in Lyon. A French bronze clock on the *fleur-de-pêche* marble mantelpiece is decorated with the familiar image of Apollo.

The smaller bedroom of William K. Vanderbilt is simply decorated in the Louis XVI style. The mantelpiece is of purple breccia marble.

The wings that hold the bedrooms of the Vanderbilt children were altered during the 1930s. Consuelo Vanderbilt's Renaissance-style suite originally included a dressing room now transformed into the Harold S. Vanderbilt Memorial Room.

In 1895, Consuelo married the ninth Duke of Marlborough against her will and at her mother's insistence. As Duchess of Marlborough she was an active supporter of social reforms aimed at helping the poor, children, and women in Great Britain. Consuelo's marriage was annulled in the 1920s following a hearing at which Alva testified to her coercive role. Consuelo's second husband was French aviator and businessman Jacques Balsan.

Just a year after Consuelo's marriage to the Duke of Marlborough, her parents were divorced. Alva, always outspoken, said, "I blazed

the trail for the rest to walk in. I was the first girl of my set to marry a Vanderbilt. Then I was the first society woman to ask for a divorce, and within a year ever so many others had followed my example." Soon after the divorce she married Oliver Hazard Perry Belmont, a friend of William K. Vanderbilt and, like him, an ardent horseman. Belcourt, his Newport summer cottage, had been designed for him by Richard Morris Hunt with elaborate stables on the ground floor. The house underwent immediate renovations at his wife's direction.

Alva continued to maintain, "I don't believe in marriage. I never shall until we have true equality of the sexes." After Belmont's death in 1908, she became increasingly active in the women's suffrage movement. She founded the Political Equality League in New York in 1909 and as its first president championed the rights of women industrial workers as well as women's right to vote. That year she also opened Marble House for a public suffrage fundraiser. In 1912 she inaugurated the Newport County Women's Suffrage League. On July 8, 1914, Alva presided over a conference of women reformers on the grounds of Marble House. Among the speakers was her daughter Consuelo who described her efforts to improve living conditions for poor and working women in England.

In 1932, just a year before she died, Alva Belmont sold Marble House to Frederick H. Prince of Boston, whose family summered in the house for thirty years. Frederick Henry Prince owned one of New England's leading brokerage firms and was president of the Chicago Junction Railways & Union Stock Yards Co. for fifty years. During his lifetime he owned a total of forty-six railroads in New York, New England, and Mexico. Soon after he bought Marble House, Prince acquired a controlling stock interest in Chicago's Armour & Co. Prince served as head of the U.S. drive for French relief during World War I, and after World War II he offered his estate at Pride's Crossing, Massachusetts, as a site for the newly created United Nations Organization. An avid sportsman, Prince distinguished himself in polo, in foxhunting in the U.S. and France (where he was master of hounds at Pau for nearly thirty years), and in yachting. Harold S. Vanderbilt was a friend of Prince and his wife Abigail Kingsley Norman—daughter of George H. Norman of Newport—and their sons. Vanderbilt often sailed the Princes' yacht *Weetamoe* which was a contender for the America's Cup defense in 1934.

Using funds provided by Harold S. Vanderbilt in memory of his mother, The Preservation Society of Newport County purchased Marble House in 1963. The Frederick H. Prince Trust donated the original Vanderbilt furnishings bought with the house in 1932.

In 1976, six years after Harold S. Vanderbilt died in Newport at the age of eighty-five, his wife Gertrude Conaway bequeathed to the Preservation Society his yachting memorabilia, collected during a lifetime of participation in the

Marble House – Alva Vanderbilt's bedroom

sport, and a number of family furnishings, including decorative arts from the Vanderbilts' Newport, Palm Beach and New York homes. A concurrent endowment made possible the creation of a Memorial Room that bears his name and celebrates his yachting career.

In 1922 Harold Stirling Vanderbilt won his first King's Cup, a gift to the New York Yacht Club from George V of England. Racing predominantly the large racing yachts of the "M" and "J" classes, he was to win six Cups in eighteen years. On Newport waters in 1925 he skippered *Vagrant* to victory in both the King's and Astor Cup races. His *Enterprise* held the America's Cup for the New York Yacht Club in 1930, winning four straight races over Sir Thomas Lipton's *Shamrock V*. In 1934 Harold's *Rainbow* was victorious against a British boat conceived by airplane designer T. O. M. Sopwith. His historic third successful defense came in the 1937 races between his "super 'J' boat" *Ranger* and Britain's *Endeavor II*. The wheel used on *Ranger*, *Rainbow*, and *Enterprise* now stands in the Vanderbilt Memorial Room. His trophies, including the seven silver-gilt King's Cups and the Astor Cup, are on display there along with drawings and photographs of Vanderbilt boats and a 1939 oil portrait by Bernard Boutet de Monvel (1884–1949) of Harold in New York Yacht Club commodore's dress at the wheel of *Ranger*.

ABOVE – Marble House – Chinese Tea House

OPPOSITE – Marble House – Chinese Tea House, interior

The Gilded Age was already waning when World War I began in Europe. The way of life associated with the Newport cottages was being replaced by a less formal and less ostentatious style, but before it was all over, Alva Belmont would make a final very visible architectural statement, a kind of exclamation point to the Gilded Age. It was the Chinese Tea House, a small, colorful oriental-style pavilion set on the cliffs behind Marble House. Richard Howland Hunt (1862–1931) and Joseph Howland Hunt (1870–1924), sons of Richard Morris Hunt, who died in 1895, designed it on the basis of their own research in the Orient. Inspired by temple buildings of southern China, the teahouse has a green-tiled roof with typically upswept eaves, half-round red pillars, and two-dozen mahogany-framed glass doors. The interior decoration includes wooden panels painted in the style of the Ming Dynasty. Although true in many ways to its models, the teahouse is a hybrid modified by a western aesthetic and built with twentieth-century western techniques.

Alva officially opened her whimsical teahouse with a lavish Chinese costume ball at Marble House in July 1914. Far too small for the hundreds who attended the ball, the teahouse served mainly a decorative purpose. The Marble House terrace, a Chinese-style footbridge over a man-made pond, the path and the teahouse itself were illuminated by Chinese lanterns and banked with exotic plants and flowers. Like many of her guests, Alva wore an antique costume imported from China. There was dancing in the ballroom of Marble House and a moonlight supper served under a huge marquee on the lawn.

The teahouse, built for small receptions and tea parties, originally stood directly above the Cliff Walk, seventy-five feet east of its present location. Moved in 1977 when the seawall became dangerously deteriorated, it was placed on a new foundation, but remained boarded up until restoration work was started in 1981. The teahouse had been exposed to the sun, wind and salt air, essentially without maintenance, for nearly seventy years. Its terra-cotta roof tiles, copper flashing and decorations, ornamental plasterwork and woodwork had been vandalized or worn by time and weather. The interior was covered with graffiti, and many of its decorative elements were missing. Using drawings made in 1912–13 by the building's architects and a number of contemporary photographs and documents, the Preservation Society restored the Chinese Teahouse to its original appearance. Plasterworkers, woodworkers, tilemakers, a painting conservator and others participated in the project, completed in 1982. That September the Chinese Tea House was officially reopened by Ambassador Chai Zemin of the People's Republic of China.

The Elms

The Elms (1901) is modeled after the mid-eighteenth-
century French château d'Asnières near Paris. The house,
designed in 1899 by architect Horace Trumbauer (1868–1938)
for coal magnate Edward J. Berwind, is a close replica of the
château designed by Jacques Hardouin-Mansart de Levy,
Comte de Sagonne (1709–1776), for the Marquis d'Argenson
in 1750.

When The Elms was completed in 1901, Berwind had
been head of the Berwind-White Coal Company for eleven
years. The firm's mining operations—directed from offices
in Boston, Philadelphia, and New York—covered more than
260,000 acres of coal lands in Pennsylvania, West Virginia,
and Kentucky, the country's largest individually owned coal
properties. Berwind-White supplied 80,000 tons of coal per
week to ships in New York harbor alone, was chief supplier to
the U. S. Navy and Merchant Marine, and had outlets along
the eastern seaboard, at Caribbean ports, and in France and
Italy. This vast company was begun by Berwind's brother
Charles and his associate Allison White in 1874.

The Berwinds were of German origin; their father, John
Paulus Berwind, was a partner in Prestien & Berwind, a
Philadelphia piano manufacturer. In 1865, seventeen-year-old
Edward was named by President Lincoln to the U.S. Naval
Academy at Annapolis. He served in the Franco-Prussian War
and was for a time a naval aide to President Grant. He left his military career for
the coal business in 1875, eventually accumulating the fortune that would bring a
French château to Bellevue Avenue, furnished with European art and antiques.

E. J. Berwind purchased a Victorian cottage known as The Elms in Newport
in 1888, just a year after his marriage to Sarah Vesta Herminie Torrey, a daughter
of a U.S. consular agent to Italy. He eventually enlarged the grounds and, in 1899,
commissioned a new house. He chose Horace Trumbauer, then a little-known
Philadelphia architect, to design it. Trumbauer was only thirty-one when he
began work on The Elms. He had served an apprenticeship in the Philadelphia
architectural firm of G. W. and W. D. Hewitt before beginning his own practice at
twenty-four. The Elms, his first major commission outside the Philadelphia area,
was followed by others in Newport, including Chetwode, Clarendon Court, and

The Elms – Garden façade

Miramar, all on Bellevue Avenue. He designed the Widener Library at Harvard University, the two main campuses of Duke University in Durham, and the Philadelphia Museum of Art.

Trumbauer's taste, like Berwinds', reflects a preference for French neoclassicism. Although he was one of the few American architects of his day not educated in Paris, his acquaintance with French architecture was obviously adequate: in The Elms he reproduced a distinguished eighteenth-century country house. Like the château d'Asnières, Edward J. Berwind's limestone cottage has a rounded central section flanked by wings of equal size, a simple classical plan of balanced proportions. Seeking to make as few changes as possible in adapting the design of the two-story château for The Elms, Trumbauer concealed the extensive staff quarters the Berwinds required behind a third-floor balustrade and arranged the

ABOVE – The Elms grand stairs

OPPOSITE – Ballroom showing Giovanni Boldini *Portrait of Elizabeth Drexel Lehr*

kitchen, laundry, and other workrooms in a deep cellar. The Elms is also raised above the ground-level situation of its model and set on a broad balustraded terrace above expansive lawns. Trumbauer manipulated the east-facing entrance façade to accommodate three towering arched doorways.

The original turn-of-the century architectural decorations of The Elms, designed by Allard and Sons of Paris, are entirely intact. The fine parquet floors, the reliefs, the ceiling paintings and elaborate moldings duplicate eighteenth-century period detailing. The similarity to the interior of Asnieres is especially apparent in the Louis XV ballroom with its graceful rounded corners and elegant white-on-ivory decorations. But The Elms is also eclectic, borrowing from a number of decorative styles in typical turn-of-the century fashion.

The ornate glass and wrought iron doors of The Elms open into a foyer with a view of the hall and ballroom. The entrance is flanked by huge rose granite urns encircled by bronze dancing nymphs. The floor in the foyer and the Great Hall it intersects is of white marble bordered in green. Ionic columns of Italian breccia marble with gilt capitals support the arcades of the hall. The doorways are framed in the same highly polished marble. Imposing ormolu and glass lanterns illuminate the hall with electric lights that originally were powered by The Elms' own generator. The eighteenth-century ordered plan of The Elms is evident beyond this hall where perfectly balanced wings extend to left and right. Throughout the house, windows are positioned to balance windows, mirrors oppose mirrors, and doors correspond to doors, creating vistas through up to four rooms at once, an effect known as *enfilade*.

In the hall facing the entry are two monumental eighteenth century Venetian paintings. Both *Scipio Declining Regal Honors* by Mattia Bortoloni (1696–1750) to the right as one ascends the entry staircase and the *Continence of Scipio* by Giovanni Antonio Pellegrini (1674–1741) opposite are from the Ca' Corner in Venice. A pair of Louis XIV-style gilt console tables with purple breccia marble tops stand beneath the paintings. They are among the original furnishings of The Elms.

Between the paintings, a double doorway with a bronze relief overdoor depicting the goddess Athena leads to the ballroom. The floorplan of The Elms is dominated by this ballroom and the salon and dining room that flank it. Cartouches over the ballroom doors frame eighteenth-century-style paintings *en grisaille*. The white stucco relief decorations of the doors, paneling, and cornice are continued in an elaborate ceiling frieze and center medallion of winged cherubs. The crystal chandelier is original to the room, as are the ormolu wall sconces, Louis XV andirons, and gilt console table. Over the console on the south wall hangs a full-length portrait of Mrs. Elizabeth Drexel Lehr by Giovanni Boldini (1842–1931).

Next to the ballroom is the dining room, decorated in Venetian style as a setting for two more grand-scale Venetian paintings. They are *Triumph of Scipio* by Angelo Trevisani (1669–1753) on the north wall and *Syphax Before Scipio* attributed to Antonio Molinari (1655–1704) on the south wall. Like the hallway paintings, they are dated 1706 and were originally part of the decoration of the Ca' Corner in Venice. The richly paneled dining room has a heavy ornamental

The Elms – Dining room

cornice and coffered stucco ceiling decorated with the Venetian lion of Saint Mark. The marble-topped sideboards supported by sphinxes and accented with gold leaf were made for the room, as were the Venetian-style dining table and chairs. An imposing ceiling-high pediment supported by carved Ionic columns frames a mantel and overmantel of agate, onyx, and marble. A bust occupies the overmantel niche. Between the opposite windows is a red marble basin with a high-relief figure of the goddess Diana.

The adjoining breakfast room is decorated in the eighteenth-century chinoiserie style. Three of the black and gold lacquer panels were made in China during the K'ang Hsi Period (1662–1722). The fourth is a nineteenth-century copy from the studios of Allard. The eighteenth-century blue and tan dragon rug is Ming Dynasty.

The Berwinds' agents procured for them a large collection of art and antique furnishings for their New York and Newport houses from sources all over Europe. Many were fine eighteenth-century originals or nineteenth-century furnishings in eighteenth-century style. Unfortunately, most of The Elms' original furnishings were dispersed at auction in 1962 before The Preservation Society of Newport County purchased the house. Some have since been restored to The Elms through gifts, loans, and purchases.

South of the central ballroom is an opulent drawing room or salon in early Louis XVI style. Musical instruments and farming motifs are depicted in wood relief over the doors. Lunettes of grey monochrome or *grisaille* on the north and south walls are framed in elaborately carved wood. Cartouches and cherubs surround a ceiling painting by Dutch artist Jacob deWit (1695–1754) of *Dawn Chasing Away the Darkness of Night*. The fine French Aubusson carpet, First Empire in style, has a design of lutes and swans.

Across the hall is the library, paneled in inlaid walnut. The walls above the wainscoting are covered in deep red damask. A carved Caen stone frame surrounds the room's walnut overmantel with its high-relief cherubs holding palm fronds. In the center is a nineteenth-century terra-cotta copy of Andrea della Robbia's Madonna and Child, in the church of San Jacopo di Ripoli in Florence. Sarah Vesta Herminie Torrey Berwind, daughter of the American envoy to Livorno, had grown up in Tuscany and later acquired a fine collection of original della Robbias and sixteenth-century Italian bronzes. They were sold along with her eighteenth-century French works of art when the Berwind estate was dispersed in 1962.

The conservatory that completes the south wing demonstrates again the opposition of mirrors, doors, and windows that gives The Elms its classical symmetry. The least formal of the house's first floor reception rooms, the conservatory has a gazebo-like ambiance, with its cool white marble floor,

The Elms – Conservatory

limestone walls, and lattice-framed mirrors; it was intended as a setting for plants and flowers. A fountain of *rouge royal* marble with a bronze group of dolphins and sea nymphs supported by sea horses stands between the east wall mirrors. Four marble sculptures, allegories of the Seasons in the room's corners are original to the conservatory. So is a prodigiously ornamented nineteenth-century marble urn adorned with full-relief satyrs, cherubs and sphynxes. The south alcove off the hallway contains a fine marble bust of a lady of the French court after the French sculptor Jean-Jacques Caffieri (1725–1792) and an important garniture of three Sèvres coral-red ground neoclassical vases decorated with panels of turks and trophies inspired by the French painter Jean-Baptiste Leprince (1734–1781). These porcelain pieces were delivered to the palace of Versailles on December 24, 1773.

The Great Hall leads back to the Grand Staircase with its white marble steps and veined breccia molding. The wrought iron and bronze railing is mid-eighteenth-century in design. Two eighteenth-century Flemish tapestries hang in the stairwell, both woven at Lille by the manufactory of Veuve de Werniers, the widow of Guillaume Werniers (d. 1738). A ceiling painting entitled *Queen Tomyris with the Head of Cyrus* was produced by Francesco Fontebasso (1709–1769) for a Venetian palazzo.

The marble floor and breccia columns of the main hall are repeated in that of the second floor, and the floor plan is nearly identical. A large family sitting room with delicate carved wood wainscoting occupies the central space over the ballroom. In this room are displayed opulent nineteenth-century French desks and seat furniture. On the floor is an excellent nineteenth-century silk Kashan palace carpet.

To the south are Mr. and Mrs. Berwind's bedrooms. The mantelpiece in Mr. Berwind's bedroom of oxblood marble, the ormolu light fixtures and red draperies are original to the room. In Herminie Berwind's much larger apartment, the walls are covered with custom-woven celadon green damask with borders of a coordinated green, gold and cream material. Both fabrics are accurate reproductions of the room's original French silks. Elaborate window hangings and bed hangings in the room are of reproduced silk *liséré*. An eighteenth-century French Regence chest stands between the west-facing windows. Above it hangs a pastel portrait of Charlotte Warren Greenough by Paul César Helleu. The bathtub and porcelain wash-stand in Mrs. Berwind's bathroom are accented in a painted laurel and swag motif.

Two small bedrooms flank the head of the staircase: the Rose Room, with French-style furniture made for the house; and the Satinwood Room, with a satin-wood bedroom suite in the style of Scottish architect Robert Adam (1728–1792) with painted decorations after the work of Angelica Kauffman (1740–1807).

The upstairs hall contains a large Italian *pietra dura* (cut-stone inlay) and *scagliola* (faux marble) center table original to the house and two rare late Gothic tapestries, from the Widener Collection, woven at Tournai during the first quarter of the sixteenth century.

A collection of British furniture gives the oak-paneled English Room (or Green Room) its name and character. An Irish Chippendale console table, a William and Mary chest-on-stand of burled walnut with seaweed marquetry, and an English Chippendale needlepoint firescreen are on display in this room.

The Van Alen Memorial Room, originally the bedroom of Edward Berwind's sister Julia, was redecorated in the 1970s as a setting for furnishings from Wakehurst, the Tudor-style Newport house of Mr. and Mrs. James Van Alen. Among the English pieces given for the room by Mr. and Mrs. William L. Van Alen are four Georgian chairs, an early nineteenth-century Sheraton breakfront, and a Sheraton secretary.

The Elms and its grounds are enhanced by a large number of stone, marble, and bronze statues and fountains. Marble sphinxes flank the front entrance, sculpture groups erected in 1903 top the parapet, and a dramatic group *Le Furie di Atamonte*, 1880, by Pio Fede (1816–1892) dominates the terrace. Half-relief statues of Aphrodite and Apollo flanking the terrace doors are castings of the restored originals from the façade of Asnières and by the sculptor Guillaume Coustou II (1716–1777), now displayed in the Conservatory. Busts of French

**Mr. and Mrs. Edward J. Berwind,
ca. 1887**

playwrights Racine and Molière on The Elms' façade are copies of the originals now placed in the library.

The Elms is distinguished by its exceptionally beautiful grounds, with their carefully clipped and shaped gingko, maple, and linden trees, massed rhododendron, and enormous weeping beeches. Ironically, the elms for which the house was named have disappeared; new trees are planted periodically in an effort to replace them.

Beyond a large bronze fountain on the broad lawn behind The Elms are the carriage house and garage built in 1911 and copied from an 1898 pavillion by the architect Henry Goury (b.1850).

Near the western edge of the eleven-acre grounds are two small marble teahouses or garden pavilions with copper roofs in the eighteenth-century French style. They mark the entrance to a formal sunken garden with hundreds of pink and white begonias and ornamental *parterre* patterns composed of miniature boxwood hedges.

Although the Berwinds were not Newport's most lavish or competitive hosts, they regularly gave dinners or balls during the summer season. Edward Berwind's work kept him in New York much of the time, but like many other summer "cottagers," he often spent weekends in Newport, traveling from Manhattan by steamer on the Fall River Line or aboard his yacht, the *Truant*. After his wife Herminie died in 1922, his sister Julia Berwind took over for him as hostess of The Elms. Edward J. Berwind died at eighty-eight in 1936. Julia Berwind summered at The Elms until her death at the age of ninety-six in 1961. She played bridge every afternoon in the conservatory, sometimes recruiting her butler to fill out the party.

In 1962, when The Elms was about to be demolished to make way for development, friends of The Preservation Society of Newport County raised money to buy it. Today, The Elms and its park-like grounds are imposing reminders of the turn-of-the-century impulse to bring the European past to life in America. In their Newport cottage, the Berwinds did more than recall the French eighteenth century; they gave form to the timeless search for beauty and excellence.

Rosecliff

A member of New York's "Four Hundred"—the city's most exclusive social circle—wrote of turn-of-the-twentieth-century Newport that "so much prestige was attached to spending July and August at the most exclusive resort in America that to have neglected to do so would have exposed a definite gap in one's social armor. It was an accepted fact that only those whose position in society was unstable never went there. Newport was the very Holy of Holies, the playground of the great ones of the earth from which all intruders were ruthlessly excluded by a set of cast-iron rules."

Among the undisputed leaders of the Newport summer colony was Theresa Fair Oelrichs. Born in 1869 at Virginia City, Nevada, to a family of ordinary means, she grew into one of the most celebrated debutantes of her day and reached her apex in Newport Society as mistress of Rosecliff.

Theresa Fair Oelrichs was an ambitious, energetic woman whose intelligence and drive were channeled into the avenue of High Society—of calling cards and invitations, dinners and balls, gowns and jewels. Her husband's niece Blanche Oelrichs wrote that Theresa "was strongly addicted to Society as a business." Everything from the elegant Daumont that carried her in Central Park's fashionable afternoon carriage procession, to Rosecliff, her regal summer house, mirrored her position and power.

Created as a showcase for extravagant summer entertainments, Rosecliff was modeled after the Grand Trianon, a baroque pleasure pavilion built in the great park of Versailles for Louis XIV by Jules Hardouin Mansart (1648–1708) between 1687 and 1691. Architect Stanford White (1853–1906) of the firm of McKim, Mead & White designed the white-glazed terra-cotta house to suit his client's turn-of-the-century requirements while preserving much of the seventeenth-century detail of its model. White's own commitment to graceful effect and beautifully sculptured ornament, evident in the finished Rosecliff, was well-known in New York and Newport circles when Mrs. Oelrichs commissioned her new summer cottage in 1898. His firm was among the most fashionable of the period.

Stanford White had entered the influential Boston architectural firm of Gambrill & Richardson at the age of nineteen. Among his assignments there was work on designs for Trinity Church in Boston and the Watts Sherman house in Newport. In 1879, after having studied in Europe, White joined C. F. McKim and W. R. Mead in a partnership that would influence the course of American architecture for decades. Among his best-known works are New York's Century Club and the neoclassical arch in Washington Square. He died tragically at fifty-three in

Rosecliff – Street façade

1906—just four years after the completion of Rosecliff—when he was shot in the roof garden of the original Madison Square Garden, a building of his own design.

Theresa Alice Fair Oelrichs, known to her friends as Tessie, was among White's most colorful clients. She was one of four children of James Graham Fair, a mining engineer who made an enormous fortune in Nevada's Comstock silver lode, and Theresa Rooney, a hotel owner's daughter from Calaveras County, California. Fair had emigrated to the United States from Ireland as a teenager and followed the Gold Rush's call to California in 1849. In partnership with three other young Irishmen, John W. Mackay, James C. Flood, and William S. O'Brien, Fair began mining on Mount Davidson in western Nevada six years after the area's silver potential was discovered. A series of fabulous strikes had already turned a tiny mining camp on the mountain into the luxurious boom town of Virginia City. Against the odds, the partners made a strike that surpassed earlier ones and earned them the title "Silver Kings." The Comstock Lode, the country's largest known silver deposit, yielded more than $500,000,000 worth of ore before it was depleted in 1898. James Fair, notorious for his lack of scruples in business, rose to respectability. He was a U. S. Senator for Nevada from 1881 to 1887, but he spent little time in Washington and spoke in the Senate only once.

Theresa Rooney Fair divorced Senator Fair on grounds of habitual adultery in 1883, twenty-one years after their marriage. She was awarded the largest divorce settlement the country had ever witnessed: $5,000,000. Her daughters Theresa and Virginia (known as Birdie) lived with her in the Fair mansion on Pine Street in San Francisco. Dark-eyed, black-haired Tessie Fair debuted there in grand style, and in 1890 was married from the house in what was reportedly the city's largest and most spectacular wedding. Her father gave her a wedding gift of $1,000,000. Her husband was Hermann Oelrichs, member of a North German family of steamship owners who had founded a branch of their business in New York in the 1840s. Gregarious and good-natured, Oelrichs was known for his humor, remarkable swimming ability, and expertise in sport fishing.

At the time of the marriage, Tessie and her sister had already been "taken up" by New York Society and had begun summering in Newport. The volatile Mrs. Oelrichs fully intended to rise to the top of East Coast Society, abandoning San Francisco and its smaller triumphs. Her husband, American agent for the North German Lloyd shipping line, was a very popular member of several fashionable New York and Newport clubs. While his wife grew more deeply enmeshed in the social competition of the East Coast, Oelrichs came to prefer the more casual social life of the West Coast, particularly San Francisco. The outcome was that he spent less and less time with his wife in the so-called "Queen of Resorts." Tessie and Hermann's only child, Herman Jr., born in 1891, grew up traveling with his mother from one "season" to another: from the Oelrichs mansion at One East 57th Street in New York, to Newport for July and August, to Saratoga, to Paris, and back to New York.

Tessie Oelrichs had access to a fortune that few, even in her exclusive set, could match. On their mother's death, Tessie and her sister had inherited a substantial fortune; three years later, in 1894, James Graham Fair died, leaving the bulk of his enormous wealth to his daughters.

The Oelrichs and Virginia Fair bought a property called Rosecliff on Newport's Bellevue Avenue from the estate of historian and diplomat George Bancroft in 1891 for $140,000. A former Secretary of the Navy, Bancroft helped found the U. S. Naval Academy at Annapolis in 1845. He served as American ambassador to England and later to Prussia, and authored a ten-volume *History of the United States* which took forty years to complete. This remarkably accomplished man devoted his leisure to two passions: horses . . . and roses. With the help of his gardener, George Bancroft surrounded his oceanside summer house with splendid rosebeds that made his favorite flower, including his triumph, the American Beauty Rose, the fashion in Newport.

For several years after they bought the eleven-acre property the Oelrichs summered in the large wood-frame house Bancroft had commissioned in 1851.

A small piece of land owned by the Parkman family stood between the Oelrichs' house and Bellevue Avenue.

A narrow service drive was Rosecliff's only connection to the avenue. In 1897, after Harry Payne Whitney (husband of Gertrude Vanderbilt) bought a neighboring property, the Oelrichs were able to acquire, with his cooperation, a strip of land wide enough to accommodate a formal entrance drive. It was then that Stanford White was engaged to design a lavish new cottage. The Parkman estate continued to separate Rosecliff from Bellevue Avenue until 1912, when Tessie Oelrichs bought it at a tax sale and made it part of her extensive west lawn.

With its gleaming white-glazed terra-cotta exterior and elegant reception rooms, Rosecliff was an appropriate setting for the woman who would plan and present many of Newport's legendary balls and dinners. The numerous arched French doors and windows, Ionic pilasters and columns, entablature, and molded floral decoration of the house all show Stanford White's close attention to his model, the Grand Trianon. The floor plan, however, is greatly modified, reduced, and simplified. Unlike its rambling French counterpart, Rosecliff takes the shape of an "H," with a horizontal central section flanked by two vertical wings of equal size. The spaces between the wings are sheltered courts—on the east side of the house a terrace overlooking the ocean, on the west or entrance side an eighteenth-century-style garden. Each of the court areas serves as an extension of the vast ballroom, Newport's largest, and is connected to it by five sets of gracefully arched French doors. The entrance to Rosecliff can be distinguished from the house's series of towering windows and doors by its elaborate wrought iron grillwork. In an attempt to adapt the look of the single-story Grand Trianon, White made Rosecliff's second story only ten feet tall, half the height of the first, and concealed the unobtrusive third-floor staff quarters behind the balustrade.

The original white-glazed terra-cotta surface of the house was restored in 1979–80. Water seepage had deteriorated the blocks of the facing and cornice; they were resurfaced or, where necessary, replaced with precast units. The balustrade, never properly secured in the rush to complete the house in 1901–02, was restored and carefully secured. Terrace paving was restored in 1983–84.

Like many elaborate houses of its period, Rosecliff was inspired by period European models but built using the technology of its own time. In everything from its steel beam construction to its plumbing and electrical systems, Rosecliff is as modern as Stanford White could make it. Norcross Bros. Inc., of Worcester, Massachusetts, was responsible for the construction of the house, and Allard and Sons of Paris and New York was engaged, as it had been at Marble House, The Breakers, and The Elms, to design the primary interiors.

Rosecliff – Grand staircase

Rosecliff is entered through a large vestibule paved with white marble. The ornately carved plasterwork, also near-white in color, was derived from eighteenth century interpretations of Palladian decoration. A lofty Palladian arch supported by columns marks the entrance to the stairhall where White's elegant rococo staircase rises on the south wall. The broad curved steps become successively narrower as they approach the first landing with its exceptionally tall arched balcony window. From there the stairway breaks into two curving sections leading to the second floor hall. A delicate black wrought iron railing follows the flowing curve of the pale Caen stone staircase.

In Tessie Oelrichs' time, the white vestibule and stairhall were furnished with massive Louis XIV gilt tables and chairs upholstered in fabric of pale rose velvet, the same color that draped the windows and carpeted the floor. A profusion of flowering plants and potted palms stood in the vestibule.

The stairhall leads to the salon or reception room, dominated by a French neo-Renaissance chimneypiece made of colored plaster. It is cast from a sixteenth-century Renaissance chimneypiece from Rouen now at the château d'Ecouen, France. The Corinthian pilasters of the walls are rococo in feeling, while the carved coffered ceiling is neo-classical. The walls above the low wainscoting, designed to be fitted with tapestries, are covered today with peach damask. Several large paintings in the room are portraits of prominent figures in turn-of-the-century Newport and New York Society.

The Louis XIV-style ballroom, originally referred to as the living room by Stanford White, is forty feet wide and eighty feet long, still unsurpassed in size in Newport. Its magnificent arched doors were opened during parties and balls to the formal garden on the west and the oceanside terrace on the east. A large white pipe organ installed at the south end of the room in 1904 was removed sometime after 1940. The French marble mantelpiece of the north wall fireplace is surmounted by a copy of an early eighteenth-century painting by Jean Antoine Watteau (1684–1721) called *Fête Champêtre* or *Country Feast*. It sets the light eighteenth-century mood of the room which is especially apparent in the splendidly decorated ceiling. Carved and molded plaster decorations surround a large

Rosecliff – Salon chimneypiece

central ceiling painting of clouds in a blue sky and twelve smaller round panels of flowers and the continents. The crystal and ormolu chandeliers are original to the room.

As at The Elms, doors have been arranged to create vistas from the salon and stairhall through the ballroom to the billiard room and anteroom in the north wing. The last two rooms were built with lower ceilings than the rest to accommodate a mezzanine level of service areas between them and the second floor.

The Louis XVI dining room originally incorporated decorative landscape paintings inset into moldings. Today the walls above the wainscoting are simply painted. Tessie Oelrichs originally furnished the room with a large white oval dining table, side tables and chairs in the Louis XVI style. The carved marble mantelpiece, the *bronze doré* and crystal chandeliers made in France were installed when the house was built.

The billiard room, later converted to use as a library by Mr. and Mrs. J. Edgar Monroe, was apparently decorated to suit the tastes of Hermann Oelrichs. The wooden mantel-piece with its small heads and caryatids echoes the Elizabethan mood of the room's walls, paneled in bleached English oak.

It is not certain which second-floor bedrooms were used by Tessie and Hermann Oelrichs during their first years at Rosecliff, but it seems likely that they occupied the north wing suite—the west bedroom was probably hers, the east one with a view of the ocean, his. In later years, when she spent nearly all of her time in the house, Tessie used the warm, bright southeast bedroom to the right at the top of the grand staircase. The smaller bedroom to the left of the stairhall was used by her son, Herman Jr.

All of the second floor bedrooms are restrained in their decoration; they have square-headed windows, simple cornices and moldings, and low French marble mantelpieces. Mrs. Oelrichs originally furnished them with walnut

Rosecliff – Ballroom

and mahogany furniture in French Empire style. They are interconnected by passageways lined with built-in closets and linen drawers which today display rotating costume exhibitions drawn from the Preservation Society's collections. The large adjoining baths, furnished with massive porcelain fixtures, have been modernized.

The third-floor staff quarters originally held ten small bedrooms, baths, and a large chamber where laundry was dried and ironed.

Tessie Oelrichs had a reputation for beauty, energy, and volatility. She dressed like a queen, according to Blanche Oelrichs, in white lace dresses and "towering picture hats," but ran her household like a tyrant, often calling for a mop and bucket to improve with her own hands the work of one of her maids.

Theresa Fair Oelrichs seated in her rose garden with her son Herman Oelrichs, Jr. and her nieces Muriel Fair Vanderbilt and Consuelo Fair Vanderbilt; ca. 1912

Her contemporaries were reportedly awed by her "racy and unfailingly amusing monologues and up-to-the-minute profanity." She also inspired many Newport legends. Her entertainments were intended to exceed the expectations of a jaded summer colony . . . and they did.

The first one opened Rosecliff in August of 1900. Mrs. Oelrichs had moved in despite the fact that the house would not be fully completed for two years, and she asked Hodgson, Newport's society florist, to disguise the unfinished state of the house. He did, with great banks of ferns, palms and flowers. More than 100 guests watched a quadrille specially choreographed for the occasion by Tessie and her friend Alva (Vanderbilt) Belmont. In August 1904 Tessie's celebrated *Bal Blanc* highlighted the week of the Astor Cup Race. Everything from the floral decorations to her own magnificent lace dress embroidered with silver mirrored the white motif the hostess had chosen for the ball. Her sister Virginia, who had married William Kissam Vanderbilt II (son of Alva and William K. Vanderbilt of Marble House) in 1899, received guests with Tessie amid banks of white hydrangeas, roses, orchids, and lilies of the valley. The east lawn fountain was stocked with swans, and a mock fleet of specially-constructed white ships floated on the waves at the base of the cliffs.

Tessie Oelrichs continued to make Rosecliff the scene of fabulous events—featuring amusements from ballet and opera to an entire circus—until Newport's Gilded Age ended with the outbreak of World War I. Hermann Oelrichs died in September 1906 of a heart attack while on a transatlantic voyage. His widow and son spent far more time in Newport and Paris than in New York. Tessie Oelrichs was blinded in one eye in a household accident in the early 1920s. Not long afterwards, she experienced a mental breakdown and was confined to Rosecliff under continuous medical care. The world in which she had debuted and later gained a leading role had disappeared; the introduction of income taxes in 1913 and changes wrought by the Great War had swept that world away like so many rose petals. Blanche Oelrichs wrote that her aunt spent her last years at Rosecliff in the company of imaginary guests, inviting them to stay just a little longer . . . to take one more glass of champagne. She died in 1926.

Tessie's son Herman continued to occupy Rosecliff in the summers until 1941. The house was sold that year to Anita Niesen, who made a gift of it to her daughter, singer and actress Gertrude Niesen. The price was $21,000. During the following winter, when the house was unoccupied, the furnace failed, water pipes froze and burst, and Rosecliff was inundated with ice. Ray Alan Van Clief bought the house the following year. He commissioned repairs to the damaged floors and ceilings and had the house refurnished. But en route to Newport, where his household staff had everything at Rosecliff prepared for his first stay, Van Clief was fatally injured in an automobile accident.

Mr. and Mrs. J. Edgar Monroe of New Orleans then purchased Rosecliff, restored it, and summered there for twenty-five years. Mr. Monroe owned extensive oil lands and sugar plantations in Louisiana. He was also president of the Boland Machine Manufacturing Co., a director of fruit, electric and realty companies, and chairman of the Canal Bank and Trust Co. Mr. Monroe and his wife Louise Stringer Monroe owned homes in New Orleans, on the Gulf Coast of Mississippi, and in Maine when they purchased and redecorated Rosecliff in 1947. They made it once again the scene of parties and dinners for hundreds of guests. In August 1971, the Monroes gave Rosecliff, its furnishings, and a trust fund for its maintenance to The Preservation Society of Newport County.

Some of the splendor of Rosecliff's Gilded Age past was recreated when the house was used as a setting for scenes from the films *The Betsy* (1973) with Sir Laurence Olivier, and *The Great Gatsby* (1974) with Robert Redford. In 2007, it appeared in the film *27 Dresses*.

In Tessie Oelrichs' day, Rosecliff was surrounded by magnificent rose gardens at which "no one glanced, save the gardener," according to Blanche Oelrichs. One of these, the five-bed south garden, was restored in 1976. Nearly 200 hybrid tea rose bushes and everblooming climbers now flower there every summer. And Rosecliff is fittingly the site of the the Preservation Society's annual Newport Flower Show.

Chateau-sur-Mer

Chateau-sur-Mer is a fascinating Victorian amalgam: a product of two periods, the 1850s and the 1870s, and a bridge between the smaller-scale early picturesque houses like Kingscote and the palatial aspect of Marble House and its Gilded Age successors. It combines the work of a Newport contractor, Seth Bradford (1801–1878), with later modifications by architect Richard Morris Hunt (1827–1895) whose work in the 1880s and '90s would help change the face of New York City's Fifth Avenue as well as that of Newport.

The story of Chateau-sur-Mer begins with William Shepard Wetmore (1801–1862), whose business career began with the Providence China Trade firm of Carrington & Co. At nineteen he sailed to Canton as supercargo of one of the company's merchantmen. Three years later, in 1823, he joined in establishing a trading company in Valparaiso, Chile. Alsop, Wetmore & Cryder became the port's exclusive agent for British and American trade and made the fortunes of its founders. In 1834 Wetmore formed a China Trade company and in a few years made it one of the largest foreign houses in Canton. He retired from international trade with a very large fortune around 1840 and four years later became a founding partner in Wetmore & Cryder, a New York banking firm associated with the London-based American banker George Peabody. (Peabody's investment house eventually became J. S. Morgan & Co., later Morgan, Grenfell & Co. of London, which helped raise funds for the Allies during World War I).

Wetmore, who owned a great deal of real estate in New York, Ohio, and Tennessee, began buying land in Newport in 1840 but did not build on it until 1852. When Chateau-sur-Mer was completed, Wetmore retired there with his wife, Anstice Derby Rogers and children, William Shepard Jr., George Peabody, and Annie Derby.

The acreage on which the rough-cut granite retreat, its brown-stone carriage house, porter's lodge, and arched entry gate were built provided an unimpeded view of the ocean to the south and southeast. Pastureland occupied what space intervened between the Wetmore property and the sea. The Chinese-style moongate still in place in the

ABOVE –
Chateau-sur-Mer
Street façade

LEFT –
Chateau-sur-Mer
ca. 1860

Chateau-sur-Mer – Grand stair

south wall framed a sea vista when it was constructed in 1860.

Chateau-sur-Mer reflected the 1850s' prevailing taste for mass and stability in residential and public buildings, and Richard Morris Hunt's later alterations did little to change the fortress-like character of the house. The original roofline is mirrored in that of Bradford's 1852 porter's lodge, a hipped gambrel with a gently outward-curving lower slope. The present much steeper Second Empire mansard roof is part of Hunt's 1872 attempt to, in the words of his wife Catherine, "bring some architectural feature out of the original impossible stone structure."

William Shepard Wetmore died in 1862, survived by two of his three children: Annie Derby Wetmore and George Peabody Wetmore. The son named for Wetmore's friend and business associate was only sixteen when he became master of what was at the time "the most substantial and expensive residence in Newport" (William P. Clark, 1877). With it came one of New York's most substantial fortunes.

Six years later, having graduated from Yale and Columbia Law School, George Peabody Wetmore was admitted to the bar in Rhode Island and New York. In 1869, he married New York and Newport resident Edith Malvina Keteltas and set off on a European sojourn that was to last, on and off, for most of the decade.

By 1871, Richard Morris Hunt had already been commissioned to provide plans for large-scale renovations and additions to Chateau-sur-Mer. When the project was completed in 1880, the house was significantly transformed. Although elements such as the 1852 porch with its wooden support posts and concave canopy remained in place, and Hunt had maintained the form of surface decoration established by Bradford, some people believed the original Chateau-sur-Mer had been demolished and replaced.

When the Wetmores returned to Chateau-sur-Mer, they settled into surroundings that reflected the most fashionable French, British, and Italian design concepts of the time. Hunt had paneled the new galleried three-story entrance hall, the grand stairway and the Morning Room with massive carved and incised white oak wainscoting and other woodwork, boldly joinered in a style inspired by the design principles of English painter and critic Charles Locke Eastlake (1793-1865).

The stairway, considered one of the most successful of Hunt's career, is enhanced by stained glass landing windows by W. J. MacPherson Co. of Boston and French bronze figures of Japanese influence. A painting on plaster of a Tree of Life extends up three flights on the underside of the grand stairs, culminating in a bird-filled sky. Charles Salagnad of Paris painted the stairwell's art—imitating a tapestry. To make his forty-five-foot high central hall appear loftier, Hunt made

ABOVE – Chateau-sur-Mer Library

OPPOSITE – Dining Room sideboard carved by Frullini

the spaces between the balconies of the second and third floors successively
narrower and installed in the ceiling a still slightly narrower stained glass panel
lighted from above by gas jets.

The Morning Room is furnished with white oak Eastlake tables, chairs, and
bookshelves designed by Hunt to coordinate with the massive beams and wainscoting, identical to that of the hall and stairway. The Morning Room was used
as a sitting room and additional library by George Peabody Wetmore. The large
fireplace is faced inside and out with Minton panels and tiles produced for it by
English painter and illustrator Walter Crane (1845–1915).

The appointments of the adjoining library were produced in the studios of
Luigi Frullini (1839–1897) in Florence, Italy, and installed at Chateau-sur-Mer in
1877–78. Predominantly Renaissance Revival in character, Frullini's richly carved

woodwork, bookcases, library table, desk and coffered ceiling are the antithesis of Hunt's Eastlake-inspired designs. The Florentine designer had previously collaborated with Hunt on Linden Gate, the Marquand estate in Newport. Frullini also designed the sumptuous dining room, with its hunting and winemaking motifs and complexity of patterns and textures. Above the burl-walnut wainscoting carved with fruit and flower designs, the walls are covered with stamped, gilded and painted leather. The floor is an elaborate herringbone parquet making complex use of several differently shaded woods. A Bohemian-majolica tile surround decorates the fireplace; a companion plaque showing a boar hunt with a seventeenth-century aspect is set into the sideboard. The table and chairs upholstered in decorated leather were made for the room by Frullini. Eighteenth-century-style cherubs in high relief cavort amid grapes and wine barrels on the massive overmantel. The grapevine motif is repeated in the Circassian walnut ceiling surrounding a large canvas that depicts George and Edith Wetmore's daughter Edith at age four in the midst of champagne-drinking cherubs.

The only first-floor interior unaltered by the renovations was the Louis XV Revival ballroom designed for William Shepard Wetmore in 1853 by New York-based French cabinetmakers Léon Marcotte and Ringuet LePrince. Painted in several shades of pale grey accented with gold leaf, the room is still furnished with pieces from the original Marcotte suite of ebonized sofas and chairs in yellow brocade. The two large mirrors and chandeliers by Cornelius & Baker, Philadelphia, are said to have been exhibited at the Crystal Palace Exposition in London in 1851.

George Peabody and Edith Keteltas Wetmore had spent most of their ten-year stay abroad in England, where they were introduced to the Arts and Crafts style of decoration promoted by designer and poet William Morris (1834–1896) and his colleagues in the English Aesthetic Movement. The goal of Morris and his associates was to fuse the fine and applied arts to produce distinctive interiors and furnishings in which form was determined by function. Their skillful designs made use of fine materials and demanded a standard of quality comparable to that of the medieval artisans whose work inspired them. The stylized patterns of their wallpapers, fabrics, and other accessories were often drawn from Gothic or oriental models. The Wetmores had several second floor rooms decorated in the Aesthetic mode, with painted and stencilled ceilings and rich stylized wallpapers and friezes. Among them are the couple's respective bedrooms, the Butternut Room, and what is now called the Turkish Sitting Room.

In the course of a decorating campaign of their own in the 1930s, Wetmore daughters Edith Malvina Keteltas and Maude Alice Keteltas nearly eliminated some of these fine interiors, having the walls, woodwork, and decorated ceilings

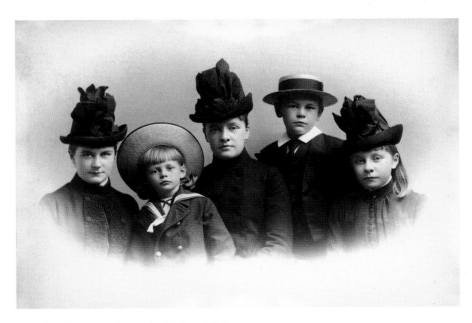

Mrs. G. P. Wetmore (center) with her children:
Edith, Rogers, William and Maude; ca. 1886

covered with oil-base paint. The Preservation Society has since restored the
rooms to their 1870s appearance. The French and English wallpapers were
reproduced on the basis of samples the Wetmore sisters had placed on deposit at
the Cooper-Hewitt, the Smithsonian Institution's National Museum of Design.
Numerous hand-cut screens were used to reproduce the elaborate stylized
patterns, some inspired by dress brocades or richly colored oriental designs.

The original painted and stencilled ceilings, some discovered only after layers
of paint were removed, were painstakingly restored with colors specially mixed to
match the originals and adjusted to reflect the age of the rooms.

Two suites of Renaissance Revival bedroom furniture commissioned from
Léon Marcotte by George Peabody Wetmore have been in place in the house
since 1869. One is the eleven-piece Eastlake-inspired butternut wood suite monogrammed "G. P. W." that gives the Butternut room its name. The other was made
for Wetmore's sister Annie (who soon after married William Watts Sherman) of
burled walnut and maple.

George Peabody Wetmore's bedroom was not redecorated in the 1930s.
The red-stained and ebonized mahogany furniture and coordinated overmantel,
made by Gregory & Co. of London in 1876, are all original to the room, as are
the painted ceiling, gilt soffit, frieze, and wallpaper. While the decorated ceiling,

French wallpaper, and frieze of his wife's adjoining bedroom are careful reproductions, much of the room's furniture and the remarkably preserved Belgian lace curtains are original.

Following his return from Europe in 1880, George Peabody Wetmore established his family in winter quarters in New York and continued to make frequent trips abroad, but he made Newport his place of legal residence. With the renovated Chateau-sur-Mer as his local base, Wetmore entered Rhode Island's political scene. A Republican, he served two terms as Governor of Rhode Island and three as a U. S. Senator from the state. In Washington he served on planning commissions for the Lincoln and Grant memorials and supported completion of the Capitol. As chairman of the Library Appropriations Committee, he was an effective advocate of the Library of Congress and its collections.

Wetmore continued to make changes at Chateau-sur-Mer throughout his life. He commissioned Richard Morris Hunt for a second, more modest, building campaign in 1882, adding a floor above the dining room wing and lifting sections of the roof. Interior designer Ogden Codman (1868–1951), a cousin of the Wetmores, was engaged in 1897 at the request of Wetmore's daughters to redecorate the drawing room, now known as the French Salon. Codman applied there the Louis XV and XVI design concepts outlined in his *The Decoration of Houses*, written with Edith Wharton and published that year. The room's delicate white Louis XV *boiseries* frame panels of green brocade are reproduced from the original silk fabric.

In 1914, John Russell Pope (1874–1937), who later designed the National Gallery of Art in Washington, was engaged by the Wetmores. Hunt's 1872 porte-cochère had been used for some time as the main entrance to Chateau-sur-Mer, eliminating the need for a doorway into Bradford's original hall. Among other changes, Pope replaced the doorway into what is now the Marble Hall with a large rectangular bay window, thereby transforming the original entrance hall into a gallery. The stencilled, painted, and gilt Japanese Revival ceiling dates from Hunt's 1870s renovations, but the wainscoting and trim of dark mahogany and the octagonal white and black marble tiles of the floor were installed when the house was built in 1852.

Around 1920, William Shepard Wetmore's original greenhouses, palm houses, and graperies were torn down, an indication that both house and family were moving into a new age. The graperies had been famed in the 1850s for the quality of their black Hamburg grapes; 250 pounds of them had been served at a single party, a *Fête Champêtre*, given on the Chateau-sur-Mer grounds in 1857. Newspaper accounts numbered the guests at 3,000, including the guest of honor, William Shepard Wetmore's friend and business associate George Peabody. The grapes were one of fifty refreshments offered, from pickled oysters to *charlotte russe.*

George Peabody Wetmore retired from public life in 1913 and died eight years later. His two sons, Rogers and William Shepard Keteltas Wetmore, died rather young, but his daughters lived long enough to be regarded as the last survivors of their "set." After the death of their mother in 1927, Maude and Edith Wetmore continued to divide their time between Chateau-sur-Mer, their New York apartment, and travel in the Orient and Europe, always a staple of Wetmore family life.

Born to one of Rhode Island's wealthiest and most influential families, Edith and Maude grew up during the years when Newport was becoming a fashionable resort for the very rich. They knew both the Newport of the 1870s and '80s, where wit and culture still sometimes opened more doors than money could, and the turn-of-the-century city where fortune and pedigree, preferably in combination, cleared the way to social prominence. When Maude died in 1951, Edith remarked, "There's no use talking about it; we're the end of an era." They were among the last representatives of the Gilded Age to be taught French by their nursemaids before they spoke English, to debut in an elite and unchallenged society, to have as birthright not just money but what Maude called "cachet."

Maude was active all her life in state and national politics. She held office in the Women's National Republican Club, the National Civic Federation, and the American Women's Association, and was an outspoken anti-prohibitionist.

On her death at ninety-eight in 1966, Edith Wetmore left a number of extraordinary nineteenth and twentieth century paintings and drawings, many bequeathed to Yale. She also left a collection of fine eighteenth century European porcelains that extended the range of the Chinese porcelain collection her grandfather had gathered during his years in the export trade. They were sold when the estate was dispersed.

The furnishings and contents of Chateau-sur-Mer were put up at auction in 1969. Key pieces were purchased by The Preservation Society of Newport County or donated, following the auction, by friends. Chateau-sur-Mer was bought by the Preservation Society the same year. Though stripped of its furnishings before the sale, Chateau-sur-Mer is today outfitted with many pieces designed for the house.

Chateau-sur-Mer is preserved today as one of the country's finest examples of Victorian architecture. The house and its furnishings crystallize in a unique form the impact of over a century's worth of design trends on a family of educated and cosmopolitan taste.

KINGSCOTE

In September of 1839, George Noble Jones of Savannah, Georgia, wrote from Potter's Boarding House in Newport to Richard Upjohn (1802–1878), founder of the American Institute of Architects and a major promoter of the Gothic Revival style in the United States, asking him to send "a plan of a cottage containing eight chambers, besides two or three sleeping apartments for servants." He added the request, advanced for the time, that "the water closets be in the house—also a bath." Neither man could have known that the cottage Upjohn designed for Jones would come to represent Newport's transition from a city struggling to overcome the effects of post-revolutionary economic collapse to a thriving cosmopolitan resort.

Traditionally, Southern and Caribbean planters and merchants had made Newport their respite from the heat of tropical summers. Newport's setting was bucolic, cooled from three sides by ocean breezes and apparently free of the disease-carrying insects that plagued the South. Even its fogs had earned the reputation of beautifying the complexion. Southern planters also found the city congenial in other ways—many Newport families held large farms and contingents of slaves to work them in neighboring towns and lived very much like their landed counterparts in Virginia and the Carolinas. After the hiatus of the Revolution and the War of 1812, the Southern contingent of summer visitors returned to Newport in force. Most stayed in small hotels or private boarding houses or rented individual cottages on the grounds of those establishments; these last were the original Newport "cottagers." Members of George Jones' family were among the regular seasonal visitors. Jones himself married a Newport woman, Delia Tudor Gardiner, in the 1830s, but she died five years before the Bellevue Avenue cottage was built. Jones was among the first to build a Newport cottage exclusively for his personal summer use and to choose what was at the time an out-of-town setting. Kingscote helped put Newport on the road to becoming America's premier summer resort.

The house was completed in 1841, the year when Newport's first major resort hotel, the Greek Revival Ocean House, was being built across the street on Bellevue Avenue.

With its asymmetry and variety of textures—its gables, dormers, pendants, bargeboards, dripmouldings, and lattices—Kingscote is an outstanding example of Gothic Revival architecture. It is, in fact, one of the few surviving wooden structures of its size, style, and period in the United States. The Gothic Revival, which began in England in the mid-eighteenth century, was in part a reaction

ABOVE – Kingscote – South façade

BELOW – David King, Jr. and family at Kingscote ca. 1878

against the stark geometric forms and grand scale of Greek Revival architecture. The style favors a smaller, more human scale, a wide variety of form and decoration, and relies heavily on organic inspiration. Although sometimes large in size, the buildings strive to be picturesque rather than impressive. It was among the first movements to directly relate houses to their surroundings. Landscape design was correlated with architecture, usually drawing the house more closely into its setting with heavy use of vines and trellises.

Even today, Kingscote has the intimacy and secluded character of the English summer retreats that inspired it. Although it is located on one of Newport's busiest streets, the grounds—one half a city block of lawn, large old trees, and shrubs—preserve some measure of the romantic natural setting its builders intended for it. The interplay of design and setting is particularly obvious in Kingscote's twin drawing rooms, where large windows open onto a veranda facing the shaded east lawn.

Kingscote's exterior surface of horizontal matched boards was originally covered with beige paint mixed with sand and scored to resemble masonry. Newport carpenter William Weeden built the house from Upjohn's plans. The grounds were laid out in the style advocated by Andrew Jackson Downing (1815–1852), author of the influential *Landscape Gardening Adapted to North America* (1841) and designer of the White House and Capitol grounds.

George Noble Jones was newly married to Mary Savage Nuttall of Florida when he moved into his ornamental cottage in the summer of 1841. The Newport

social life the Joneses enjoyed was relatively informal, relaxed, and oriented to the outdoors: horseback riding on the beaches, carriage driving and racing, archery, croquet, walking. Swimming was a popular pastime both at First Beach, where only women bathed in the mornings and only men in the afternoons, and at exclusive Bailey's Beach, where the bold step of tolerating mixed bathing had already been taken.

Mary Edith Powel, a neighbor and friend of the Jones family, recorded her childhood memories of Kingscote where she was a frequent visitor during the 1850s. Interiors, she wrote, were simple and refined, with nothing of "overdone luxury," and an abundance of sunlight, "very little incommoded by a few Nottingham lace curtains." Over the front door of the house was an aviary—a sort of bow window room full of birds—gorgeous macaws, parrots, and others all quite big and all screeching at once. And she recalled the sound of the sea as "very near then . . . with little hindrance from street or cottage between us and the ocean."

ABOVE – Kingscote Library
OPPOSITE – Stair Hall

After a trip to Europe in 1856, the Joneses returned to find Newport tenser—with a growing summer population of Bostonians, many of them abolitionists—and more crowded, with cottages proliferating in Kingscote's once isolated quarter. The family was already spending far less time in Newport when the Civil War severed their ties to the city. Six months after the war began in 1861, Jones transferred title to Kingscote to prevent its confiscation and shipped most of its contents to Georgia. As a result, very few of the furnishings at Kingscote today can be positively dated to the Jones period. On April 29, 1863, the cottage was sold to William Henry Hunter King, a relation of the family for which Hunter House was named, for $35,000.

Edward LeRoy King, William's brother, lived just west of Kingscote's property line in an Italianate villa designed for him by Upjohn in 1845. During his frequent stays there William had become a friend of the Jones family and had cared for their cottage during their long absences in the 1850s and early 1860s.

The Kings were not new to Newport. The grandfather of Edward and William

Kingscote – South Parlor

King had established a medical practice in the city late in the eighteenth century. Their father, Dr. David King, also a respected physician, was a stockholder in Russell & Co., a major American China Trade firm. The family's connections to China shaped King lives for several generations.

When William Henry King was twenty-two years old, he was sent to China to learn the export trade in which his older brother Edward was already well established. While he began his work in the tea trade reluctantly, William soon showed a talent for the business and his fortunes rose quickly. He was a partner in Russell & Co. by the time he was twenty-five. At thirty-two he was a very wealthy man, wealthy enough to leave the China Trade—and his stations at Canton and Macao—and return to Newport where he hoped to settle permanently near his family. An oil-on-ivory miniature portrait painted by Richard M. Staigg (1817–1881) at the time of William's retirement in 1850 is on display at Kingscote.

When William settled in the whimsical cottage neighboring his brother's monumental ltalianate villa, he brought with him many of the Chinese porcelains, paintings, and furnishings that decorate the house today. William's interest in painting is evidenced in his accumulation of Chinese works, one of the largest private collections still intact. Among the paintings are several produced especially for export to the West by Chinese artists of the school of British expatriate artist George Chinnery (1774–1852): views of Canton harbor, Cantonese street scenes, views of Macao, and others. A portrait above the library fireplace of Houqua, senior Chinese Hong merchant and a friend of the King family, was a gift to William King upon his retirement from the China Trade. King also brought to the house his eighteenth and nineteenth century Chinese Export porcelains and Dutch Delftware inspired by the blue and white scheme of Chinese models.

William Henry King changed the aspect of his cottage very little—he may have had it painted in charcoal grey with red and black trim in 1864, or that may have been done somewhat later by his nephew. After two years of living and entertaining in grand style at Kingscote, King experienced a mental breakdown from which he never recovered. From 1866 until his death thirty-one years later he lived in mental hospitals, and Kingscote was administered by Newport's Probate Court through a succession of guardians—all family members. Probate records detail expenses for upkeep, renovations, and furnishings, as well as income from rental of the house between 1866 and 1897. Among the expenses are items sent to William at McLean Hospital in Massachusetts and Butler Hospital in Providence: books, flowers, music boxes, imported cigars, and a Brewster brougham.

David King Jr., who took over the guardianship in 1875, was the first relative to rent Kingscote from his Uncle William's estate. After an unpromising school career, David had begun his business life at seventeen as a clerk for a New York importing firm. In 1858 he went to China to work for Russell & Co. as his uncles had done. A sepia photograph at Kingscote shows him standing on the porch of the company's "hong" or trading house in Canton. He retired with a comfortable fortune at the age of thirty-four. Widowed after a brief first marriage, David King Jr. married Ella Louisa Rives of Virginia and Newport, an intelligent and lively woman known for her skill at horsemanship and her mastery of languages. Within a few years of her marriage, Ella King encouraged her husband to reno-vate Kingscote, which she found charming if somewhat dated, for their own use.

To accommodate the increasingly formal tastes of post-war Newport—where a social style imported from the large Eastern cities was displacing the rustic amusements of the 1850s—the Kings redecorated, restocked kitchen and pantry, and made room for a growing household. Newport architect George Champlin Mason (1820–1894) designed a modest addition, expanding the dining room and staff quarters, that was completed in 1878. The wallpaper of this "old" dining room (now the library) is an example of the English Aesthetic Movement designs of William Morris (1834–1896). It dates from Mason's addition as do the carved mahogany mantelpieces of the library and front parlor. The circa 1840 rococo marble mantelpiece of the back parlor, removed from a New York City property owned by the family at 8 Washington Place, was also installed at this time. The only mantelpiece dating from Kingscote's construction in 1841 is that of the second floor southeast bedroom. Its Tudor arch is typical of Upjohn's modest woodwork designs for the house, evident in the entrance hall and twin parlor archways.

The Kings had stained glass made by Friedrich Brothers installed in place of the original entrance hall sidelights; oak parquet floors were laid in the hall and twin parlors. A great deal of new furniture was purchased, including pieces from the fashionable New York design firm of Léon Marcotte. A June 1878 entry in the Newport probate records shows a payment of $1,155.45 to the company for "sundry furniture" which probably included the overstuffed Turkish-style suite of sofas and chairs, upholstered in rose damask, that is still in place in Kingscote's south parlor. The flocked green wallpaper in the same room was also bought from Marcotte.

David King brought to Kingscote his own additions to his uncle's collection of Chinese porcelain and furnishings, among them an early nineteenth century teakwood familial shrine and a four-fold teakwood screen with panels exquisitely embroidered in silk.

On June 1, 1880, David King's "Gothick" cottage was officially registered for the first time under the name of Kingscote. He was living there with his wife, their two small children, and a staff of ten, from butler to nursemaid. This establishment continued to grow as Newport summer life came to conform more closely to the rigid formal standards of New York Society. A spirit of competition and a taste for display transformed the entertainments of the summer community and changed the nature of its cottages. In 1881, King commissioned the newly formed firm of McKim, Mead & White of New York to design a three-story addition to Kingscote, incorporating a spacious dining room on the ground floor, a hall and two bedrooms on the second, and children's bedrooms and a bath on the third. To make way for the enlargement, the service wing expanded in 1878 was moved back forty feet. Exterior details were made to correspond as closely as possible

Kingscote – Dining room

to Upjohn's. Although the addition's scale is disproportionately large, preserving the integrity of the house's original design was clearly a priority for King and his principal architect, Stanford White (1853–1906).

The extraordinary dining room, large enough to double as a ballroom, is by far the most lavish room in the house. White's predominately "Queen Anne" decorative scheme draws on a number of sources—Oriental, British, American, Italian—and a variety of rich textures and shadings. Mead & Taft of New York executed from White's designs the delicate removable spool and spindlework mahogany screen, the wainscoting, the silver and china cabinets, the built-in Colonial Revival sideboard and the cherry parquet floor. They covered the upper walls and ceiling with a herringbone pattern of cork acoustic tiles, among the first used in decorating.

Louis C. Tiffany & Co. (later known as Tiffany Studios) of New York produced the opalescent glass bricks and tiles and the dahlia mosaics over the Italian Siena marble fireplace. The dahlia motif is echoed in White's hammered brass wall brackets and cast-iron fireback.

The addition was completed in March 1882. The present red slate roof was installed four years later in place of what was probably a wooden shingle one.

In March 1894, David King Jr. died in his house in Washington, D.C., after an appendectomy. In 1896 his widow Ella Rives King returned from an extended stay in France and moved into Kingscote with her nineteen-year-old daughter, Maud Gwendolen King, and seventeen-year-old son, Philip Wheaton King. In August Ella King entertained 500 guests at a coming-out ball for Maud. The elaborate floral decorations of "the entire first floor" included "a miniature lake full of water lilies and lotus flowers . . . rare foliage plants reaching to the ceiling . . . banana trees . . . and rose bushes 11 feet high in full bloom."

After William Henry King's death at seventy-nine in 1897, it appeared that Kingscote would be sold and the proceeds divided among a dozen heirs. To prevent the loss of the house she found so appealing, Ella Louisa Rives King bought Kingscote from the estate for $75,000 and purchased most of the furnishings at auction. In 1900 her daughter Maud met and fell in love with Edward Maitland Armstrong of New York, son of diplomat, painter, and stained-glass designer David Maitland Armstrong (1836–1918). A bronze bas-relief portrait of the latter, made by his friend the sculptor Augustus Saint-Gaudens (1848–1907) in 1878, is on display at Kingscote, as are Armstrong's oil painting *The Chimney Corner* and examples of his work in watercolor. After a year abroad with her mother, Maud returned to Newport to marry Edward Armstrong at Trinity Church. When her husband died in 1915, Maud and her three children took up residence with her mother, who remained an avid horsewoman and international traveler until her death in 1925. Maud was enabled under the terms of her mother's will to live at Kingscote indefinitely, covering only those expenses not met by a trust fund for the property.

During the 1950s and '60s, Maud Armstrong resisted the city government's repeated efforts to buy and demolish Kingscote and build a school in its place. Her commitment to preserving architectural landmarks made her an active supporter of The Preservation Society of Newport County. Kingscote stands today, skirted by two modern shopping centers, as a monument to her foresight and endurance.

Both Maud Armstrong's sons, Maitland and David, died before their mother did—David at Kingscote in 1967, only one year before Maud's death. Kingscote was left to her remaining child, Gwendolen Ella Armstrong Rives (1911–1972).

**Mrs. Edward Maitland
Armstrong with her children
Edward, Jr. and Gwendolen**

After her marriage to second cousin Anthony George Barclay Rives, Gwendolen made her home in Virginia, but continued to share her mother's interest in antiques and historic preservation. She returned to Newport to live with Maud at Kingscote after her husband's death in the early 1960s and occupied the house for the rest of her life. When she died in 1972, she left Kingscote with its furnishings and a trust fund for its maintenance to the Preservation Society, assuring the future of the house her family enjoyed for more than a century.

Architecturally significant in its own right, Kingscote is also a museum of period interiors and decorative objects—from fine Oriental rugs to distinctive porcelains—commissioned or collected by five generations of the King family and preserved as they left them.

THE ISAAC BELL HOUSE

The Isaac Bell House is one of the best surviving examples of Shingle Style architecture in America. It was erected 1881–1883 by the firm of McKim, Mead & White as a summer residence for Isaac Bell, Jr. (1846–1881), a wealthy cotton broker and brother-in-law of James Gordon Bennett Jr., publisher of *The New York Herald*. Bennett's nearby Newport Casino was just being completed when the publisher suggested the firm of McKim, Mead & White to his sister Jeanette Bell.

The Bell house represents the zenith of nineteenth-century America's search for a national style. Blending English Queen Anne with New England colonial and Oriental design influences, the architects created a rallying point for a new "vernacular" style, a style that came to be known as the "shingle style" due primarily to the picturesque quality of exteriors sheathed in native white cedar shingles. McKim, Mead & White's designs of the 1880s are an important part of Newport's architectural evolution and were to have a significant impact on the later domestic work of Frank Lloyd Wright. After passing through a succession of owners, the house was purchased in 1994 by The Preservation Society of Newport County. In 1997, the Isaac Bell House was designated a National Historic Landmark.

Viewed from Bellevue Avenue, the entire building, apart from the brick ground floor, is faced with wooden shingles. The varied massing of projecting verandahs, twin gables, sleeping porch, ballooning tower, and salt-box service ell are unified by courses of multi-patterned shingles. Running from top to bottom they vary from a wave to scalloped-pattern, to rough-surfaced rectangles finished off with a jigsaw edge trim. Towering asymmetrical chimneys dominate the roofline, while subtle decorative nuances such as a tripartite over-window with central sunburst, faux bamboo porch columns and subtly gilded dolphin brackets at the main entrance hint at the exoticism of blending colonial design references with the flavor of the Far East.

The novelty of the Bell House's interior design is its use of an open and informal floor plan. Sliding partitions in the central living hall roll back to transform the ground floor into a single open reception space. Light oak wainscoting rises to the height of Japanese sliding partitions over which hang exposed bracing hardware stamped with a stylized chrysanthemum, symbol of the Imperial House of Japan.

Stanford White's decorative genius is visible in his use of architectural salvage from Brittany as a romantic backdrop for the cozy inglenook. Disassembled Breton box beds, armoires and cornices have been reconfigured to create an ensemble that evokes the creative possibilities of folk furniture and the

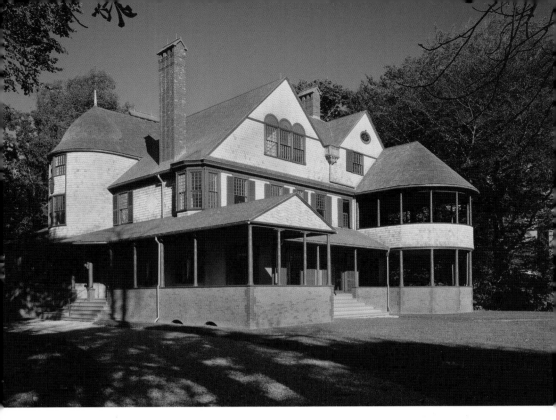

Isaac Bell House – Street façade

architectural potential of natural light. When the afternoon sun basks the west-facing inglenook, colored light from nearby stained-glass windows penetrates the dark chestnut-lined walls of the alcove via the open box bed which serves to literally frame the bouncing shafts of light.

In the adjoining dining room a more overt reference to Oriental traditions occurs with the use of natural rattan as a covering for both walls and ceiling. Framed by strips of mahogany molding, the rattan is further accentuated by inset brass brazier panels hinting at the Moorish heritage of Spain and North Africa.

The Bell family's drawing room is decorated in the pastel hue of a colonial-inspired pale green. The walls are upholstered in a curious horizontal-banded puckered silk. The flanking reception room features woodworking painted ivory and picked out, in the subtlest manner, with pencil-thin lines of gilt decoration, surrounding walls covered with a blue-on-blue Japanese-inspired silk.

Light organic colors are also used throughout the second floor family rooms, alternating with luxurious embossed French wallpapers and patterned metallic patterned papers. The whole creates, in the novelty of its informal design, a unique, if short-lived, summation of American style at a vibrant crossroad.

Chepstow

Chepstow, an 1860–61 Italianate villa, was built as a summer residence for Edmund Schermerhorn (1817–1891) and was designed by Newport architect George Champlin Mason, Sr. (1820–1894). A three-story dwelling with a low, French-style mansard roof, Chepstow has undergone several alterations but the exterior has lost little of its Italianate character, including overhanging eaves with decorative brackets, projecting entrance tower, round-headed windows with hood moldings, wrap-around verandah and balustraded balconies.

Schermerhorn, a wealthy New York bachelor, was descended from a prominent Dutch family and was the first cousin of Mrs. William Backhouse Astor, Jr. (née Caroline Schermerhorn), a leader of Newport and New York society. Mr. Schermerhorn used the villa as a summer residence for several seasons before retiring permanently to Newport. At the time of his death in 1891, he was reported to be Newport's richest year-round resident.

The property was purchased by Mrs. Emily Morris Gallatin in 1911. She named the property "Chepstow" after a castle in Wales captured by Lewis Morris in 1648 during the English Civil War. Mrs. Gallatin was a descendant of the Colonial Lords of the Manor of Morrisania, whose lands comprised more than 5,000 acres in what are now the states of New York and New Jersey, and of Lewis Morris III, a signer of the Declaration of Independence.

In 1921, the Gallatins added to the property with the purchase of the adjacent George Henry Warren estate. After their deaths, Chepstow was left to Mrs. Gallatin's first cousin, Lewis Gouverneur Morris; and his two daughters, Alletta Morris MacDonald and Frances Morris Perry.

Mrs. MacDonald and her family took possession of the house in 1950. Mrs. MacDonald, born Miss Alletta Lorillard Morris (1912–1986), was the daughter of Lewis Gouverneur and Nathalie Bailey Morris. She was introduced to New York society in 1930 and married Brynes MacDonald in 1935. Mr. MacDonald was president of the Sinclair Oil Company from 1946 until his death in 1959 at the age of fifty-one.

In 1963 Mrs. MacDonald married Peter McBean of San Francisco. The McBeans traveled extensively, returning to Chepstow every summer. Later in life, Mrs. McBean turned her love of Newport into active support of its history by becoming a trustee of The Preservation Society of Newport County. She was one of the Society's foremost contributors, and was given its most distinguished award, the Antiquarian Medal, posthumously, in June, 1986. She bequeathed Chepstow to the Preservation Society and also established the Alletta Morris

ABOVE – Chepstow street façade

BELOW – Stair Hall

McBean Foundation to "enhance the quality of life in, and perpetuate the history of, Newport."

The house contains original Morris-Gallatin furnishings together with a collection of important nineteenth-century American paintings and documents consolidated from other former Morris family residences. Its highlights include a large marinescape by Fitz Henry Lane, Hudson River landscapes by George Hardy and Thomas Doughty and portraits by Daniel Huntington. Chepstow is a highly evocative glimpse of the taste and collections of a descendant of one of America's founding families, against the backdrop of a contemporary Newport summer home.

Hunter House

The story of The Preservation Society of
Newport County begins with Hunter House. In
1945 a group of Newporters joined together to save
Hunter House from deterioration. Their efforts to
restore and preserve this distinguished example of
eighteenth-century domestic architecture led to the
formation of the Preservation Society. The careful
restoration of Hunter House, based on painstaking
research and analysis, set a precedent in preservation work both within and beyond Newport.

In the 1740s Newport was the commercial
and political capital of Rhode Island, comparable
in importance to Philadelphia, Boston, New York,
Charleston, Savannah, and Baltimore. The city
shared with Providence a lively sea trade which
included exchanging lumber, fish, and cheese for
British manufactured goods. Fewer restrictions
and greater profits resulted from the lucrative
Triangular Trade. Iron, flour, tar, and rum made
by the colony's thirty or so distillers were shipped
to Africa's Gold Coast where they were traded
for slaves. In West Indian ports, the slaves were
sold at a profit, and the ships took on cargoes of
sugar and molasses for sale to Rhode Island rum
producers. Piracy, smuggling, and privateering were
widespread, and Newport was an acknowledged
center for them. The religious tolerance on which
the colony was founded made the city a haven for
dissidents of all kinds. Quakers, Jews, and others
whose freedoms were limited elsewhere built their
enterprises without molestation.

In 1748, at the height of Newport's prosperity,
Jonathan Nichols Jr. bought a piece of land on the
bustling two-mile harborfront where merchants,
captains, shipbuilders and sailmakers had their
homes and businesses.

Hunter House – Street façade

A native Newporter with large landholdings in nearby Portsmouth, Nichols had a house, a wharf and warehouses built on the Washington Street (then Water Street) site to accommodate his shipping enterprises. He grew prosperous as the owner of ships involved in the Triangular Trade. In the course of his career, Nichols held several posts in the colonial government. At the time of his death in 1756, he was deputy governor of Rhode Island.

In 1757, the Washington Street property was sold to Colonel Joseph Wanton, Jr. Wanton had the house—a single-chimney dwelling in Nichols' time—enlarged to its present proportions. He came from a family of wealthy and influential Quaker merchants and traders; his grandfather, father, and uncle each served the Crown as governor of Rhode Island. When he and his wife Abigail Honyman moved into their new home, the Harvard-educated Wanton was firmly established in the family shipping business. In addition to his West Indian and Atlantic coast trading ventures, Wanton's father had a privileged position collecting port duties for the British, and a leverage he did not hesitate to use to screen the family's privateering operations. Widowed in 1771, Joseph Wanton married another Newport woman, Sarah Brenton, four years later. By then the political climate of Newport was running counter to his staunch Loyalist views. Wanton had served several terms in the colonial assembly and risen to the post of deputy governor when the Revolution put an end to his government career. His father was removed as governor in 1775, and Wanton himself was arrested seven months later. With the British occupation of Newport he briefly regained some influence but was forced to flee when the British left the city for New York. The French allies of the Revolution, under Comte de Rochambeau, entered Newport soon afterward. Wanton died in 1780.

The Wanton house on Washington Street, confiscated by the new state government, became for a time the residence of Admiral de Ternay, commander of French naval forces in America. Seriously ill when he arrived in Newport, de Ternay died in the house seven months later. The property continued to be used as French naval headquarters until 1781.

When the conflict ended, Newport's economy was devastated; the port fell silent and remained so for several decades. Many of the city's houses were empty; most of its residents destitute. The Washington Street house fell into disrepair and passed through a succession of owners. William Hunter saved the house from disintegration when he bought it for $5,000 in 1805. Hunter House would belong to his family for more than fifty years.

A lawyer born in Newport and educated in England, Hunter was a member of Rhode Island's General Assembly for twelve years and a United States Senator

Hunter House – Front door pediment

Hunter House – Northeast Parlor

for ten. Eight of the nine children of William and Mary Robinson Hunter were born at Hunter House. One of their sons, Charles, landscaped the grounds after removal of the old colonial-era wharf and warehouses. William Hunter enjoyed a reputation in political circles for his powerful, classic oratory; at home he was feared for his stern manner and harsh punishments.

In 1834 Andrew Jackson made Hunter chargé d'affaires to Brazil. His diplomatic mission kept him in Rio de Janeiro for the next ten years. Hunter House was leased and allowed to deteriorate. Hunter's son Thomas called it "Ricketty Hall" and urged his father to send money to restore it to "habitable condition." The necessary repairs were made only after Hunter's return to Newport. In December 1849, when he was in the process of writing a history of religious toleration in Rhode Island, William Hunter died at Hunter House.

After the Hunters sold the property in 1863, it passed through many hands. A Boston family, the Storers, purchased Hunter House in 1881 and spent summers there until 1917, when they gave the house to nearby St. Joseph's Church for use as a convent. Twenty-eight years later, Hunter House was purchased from the parish for $15,000, a sum contributed by Mr. George Henry Warren and a group of fellow Newporters; his wife Katherine Urquhart Warren helped found The Preservation Society of Newport County and served as its president and chairman of the board for many years.

Hunter House is prized for the quality of its interiors. The carved paneling, black and gold Corinthian pilasters and baseboards, shell carvings and small polychromed cherub heads of the northeast parlor are examples of the fine details in the house. It is one of five fully paneled rooms on the first and second floors. Paint colors throughout Hunter House approximate those used during the 1760s and 1770s, when the Wanton family occupied the house. The pine paneling of the southeast parlor is "grained" or painted to resemble walnut. That of the southwest room and the dining room is "spreckled" in a pattern simulating walnut. Many large eighteenth-century Newport residences had rooms similarly paneled with pine and painted to resemble more costly woods, but very few of these interiors survive. Chambers in Trinity Church (1726) and the Colony House (1739) illustrate the use of full paneling in Newport public buildings.

Several of Hunter House's twelve-paned windows have original interior shutters and mahogany window seats. The main staircase with its turned Santo Domingan mahogany balusters of three alternating designs are less classical than the woodwork of the rest of the house.

Although the three long-term owners of Hunter House are known to have purchased and used furniture produced by the celebrated Townsend and Goddard families, most of the pieces were dispersed during the long and checkered history of the house. The Preservation Society has been able through generous gifts and loans to gather for Hunter House one of the country's finest collections of period furnishings made in Rhode Island, other parts of New England, and Great Britain.

The most distinguished of Newport's eighteenth and nineteenth-century cabinetmakers, the Townsends and Goddards produced furniture valued for the excellence of its proportions, execution, and materials. Mahogany obtained at Caribbean ports—in Cuba, Santo Domingo, and Honduras—through the Triangular Trade was particularly favored. The work of the Townsends and Goddards combines elements of classical and Palladian designs, as do the carved wainscoting and pilasters of the Hunter House interiors. Examples of their craft in the Hunter House collection illustrate the features that set the Newport cabinetmakers apart: very finely rendered shell carvings, block fronts, well-defined and sometimes undercut ball and claw feet. Among the particularly notable pieces is a marble-topped side table with a serpentine front carved from a single block of mahogany. Produced by John Goddard in the 1740s, the piece is one of only a few known to have been made to hold a marble top. The extraordinary chest-on-stand of the northwest bedroom, also the work of John Goddard, combines several hallmarks: the shell-carved apron, Newport-style blocked pediment, acanthus-carved knees, and finely detailed ball-and-claw feet.

Dr. William Hunter, 1769 portrait by Cosmo Alexander

Among several important paintings at Hunter House is a rendering of two dogs of Scottish-born physician Dr. William Hunter, father of the owner of Hunter House. It was executed by Rhode Island artist Gilbert Stuart (1755–1828) and is described in a Providence exhibition catalogue of 1829 as the "first piece after the artist recovered his sight." The portraits of Dr. Hunter and his wife Deborah Malbone Hunter (a descendant of Joseph Wanton) were painted by fellow-Scot Cosmo Alexander (d. 1773), an early teacher of Gilbert Stuart, in 1769.

The exterior of Hunter House looks much as it did after Joseph Wanton had the house enlarged circa 1750. Beneath its cream-colored paint (the color first applied after many years of weathering) are clapboards of pine dating from the Nichols era and of oak from nineteenth-century repairs.

The handsome front doorway encapsulates the history of Hunter House. With its flanking classical pilasters and polychromed pineapple, the door origi-nally stood at the waterside entrance, the business side in the eighteenth century. Removed during the 1870s, the doorway was installed in a neighboring house and returned when restoration of Hunter House was initiated in 1945. The decorative

**Hunter House –
Northeast Parlor**

pineapple was a colonial symbol of hospitality that grew out of the sea captains'
practice of setting a fresh pineapple outside the door to indicate that fruit
from the West Indies was available within for anyone who cared to enter. The
Preservation Society of Newport County adopted the pineapple motif for its seal
and logo in 1947. Hunter House's fine example of this decoration today welcomes
visitors to a singular experience: a glimpse into an extraordinarily authentic
setting of colonial merchant-class domestic life.

An eighteenth-century-inspired garden and pergola present the formal
design of period Newport landscaping and were a generous gift of two friends of
The Preservation Society.

GREEN ANIMALS

I n 1872, a seven-acre estate on the shores of
Narragansett Bay in Portsmouth, not far from
Newport, was purchased by a man who wanted to
emulate ancient pharaohs and European kings. But it
was neither their power nor their palaces that interested him; it was their gardens . . . topiary gardens.

Treasurer of the Union Cotton Manufacturing
Co. in nearby Fall River, Massachusetts, Thomas E.
Brayton was fascinated with this unusual form of
gardening—training and clipping trees and shrubs
into geometric patterns and animal shapes. Topiary
reached the height of its popularity in Europe during
the seventeenth century when intricate and carefully
tended mazes and ornamental configurations of
privet, yew, and boxwood were part of the landscaping of countless palaces and country estates.

Thomas Brayton's garden surrounded a modest
dwelling—a wood-frame house built at the foot of
rural Cory's Lane circa 1860—but no less care was
devoted to it by Brayton and his gardener Joseph
Carreiro, who had learned the topiary art in his
native Portugal. Gradually they developed one
of the country's few topiary gardens and perhaps
the only one combining stylized geometric forms,
like spiraling trees, or hedges pruned to resemble
classic arches, with animal and human shapes. The
garden grew to include an assortment of roses,
boxwood-edged formal flower beds, herbs, orchards,
trellised grapevines, water lilies, berry patches, and a
vegetable garden, as well as the topiary.

Brayton's daughter Alice (1878–1972) called her
father's garden "Green Animals" and made the estate
her permanent residence after his death in 1939. She
carried on her father's work with garden superin-
tendent George Mendonca, student and son-in-law
of Joseph Carreiro. During her tenure, the topiary

Green Animals – Topiary garden

ABOVE – Miss Alice Brayton, ca. 1955

OPPOSITE – Green Animals – Topiary garden

increased to its present proportions, and her attachment to it grew accordingly. Alice Brayton was a scholar and writer as well as a horticulturist, and she was keenly aware of the need to insure the future of her gardens beyond her lifetime. She received an offer from the New York Botanical Garden to transplant the topiary to their facilities in the Bronx, but she rejected it, saying, "I couldn't bear the idea of seeing my giraffe leaving through the front gate."

Miss Alice, who wrote a number of books on historical subjects, was nonetheless energetically committed to the present. Among other involvements, she was a founder of the District Nursing Association of Fall River, Miss Alice helped begin the Newport Garden Club, worked in food distribution programs during the Great Depression, and frequently hosted members of the Washington press corps when they followed President Dwight D. Eisenhower to Newport during the 1950s. When she died in 1972 at the age of ninety-four, she left Green Animals, the Brayton house, its greenhouse, barn, and cottage to The Preservation Society of Newport County with the understanding that the gardens would be preserved and made accessible to the public.

Today more than 200 species of flowers bloom in the beds of Green Animals' gardens every year. Among them are dahlias, roses, impatiens, begonias and marigolds in numerous varieties. A magnificent magnolia arbor arches over one of the many garden paths. There are grape arbors, peach, pear, quince, and apple trees, some of them espaliered, and vegetable gardens. More than fifty different herbs are grown.

But most importantly there is Miss Alice's magical topiary, now over eighty pieces strong. More than forty-five of them are American and golden boxwood shrubs pruned and trained into arches, globes, pyramids, urns, and towering spirals. The remainder are creatures, some of them generations old.

It takes several years for a topiary figure to reach maturity, and pieces broken by weather or mishandling can take many seasons to recover. Miss Alice's giraffe, originally long-necked, was rebuilt in its present short-necked condition after a hurricane severely damaged it in 1954. New pieces are periodically added to the topiary collection.

The Brayton house containing vintage family furnishings and several publications by Miss Brayton has been, in part, adapted for use as a small children's toy museum. The displays include toys as diverse as Victorian bisque dolls with their furniture and china, a 400-piece collection of miniature lead soldiers, early twentieth-century dollhouses, and board games. One room has been outfitted as a nineteenth-century nursery with period children's clothing and accessories, furniture and china.

But the whimsical privet policeman, unicorn, ostrich, rooster, lion, dogs, donkey, and their companions remain the heart of Miss Alice Brayton's Green Animals—one of the country's most fascinating combinations of history, horticulture, and fantasy.

Photographs by Richard Cheek, John Corbett, Andrea Carneiro, Ira Kerns,
Patrick O'Connor, Stephen Mattos and Jim Patrick.
Original text by Ann Benway, revised 2012.

Designed by David Cameron.

Printed in Korea.

Published and distributed by:
The Preservation Society of Newport County
424 Bellevue Avenue
Newport, Rhode Island 02840-6924
401-847-1000

www.NewportMansions.org